THE KNOWLEDGE CIRCLE

Norse Magic and Runes

Runic Wisdom and Magic to Enhance Your Life

IPPOCERONTE
publishing

© Copyright 2022 - All rights reserved.

The content contained within this book may not be reproduced, duplicated or transmitted without direct written permission from the author or the publisher.

Under no circumstances will any blame or legal responsibility be held against the publisher, or author, for any damages, reparation, or monetary loss due to the information contained within this book, either directly or indirectly.

Cover and book formatting by thiwwy design (@thiwwy)

LEGAL NOTICE

This book is copyright protected. It is only for personal use. You cannot amend, distribute, sell, use, quote or paraphrase any part, or the content within this book, without the consent of the author or publisher.

DISCLAIMER NOTICE

Please note the information contained within this document is for educational and entertainment purposes only. All effort has been executed to present accurate, up to date, reliable, complete information. No warranties of any kind are declared or implied. Readers acknowledge that the author is not engaged in the rendering of legal, financial, medical or professional advice. The content within this book has been derived from various sources. Please consult a licensed professional before attempting any techniques outlined in this book.

By reading this document, the reader agrees that under no circumstances is the author responsible for any losses, direct or indirect, that are incurred as a result of the use of the information contained within this document, including, but not limited to, errors, omissions, or inaccuracies.

CONTENTS

INTRODUCTION 11
Who Were, or Are, the Norse? 12
Do People Still Practice Norse Magic and Read the Runes? 12
Runes Are Hidden All Around You 13
Serious Stuff Only 13

PART I - THE NORSE

CHAPTER 1
THE NORSE IN HISTORY 17
Are the Norse and Vikings the Same People? 17
Possible Cousins and Ancestors to Norse Culture 17
Ancient Scandinavian Culture 19
Through Trade and Terror: Areas of Norse Cultural Influence 20

CHAPTER 2
ANCIENT NORSE RELIGION AND RITUALS 23
The Norse Gods 24
   Odin *25*
   Frigg *27*
   Freya *29*
   Tiw *30*
   Thor *31*
   Ullr *33*
   Frey *33*
   Baldur *34*
   Loki *35*
   Njord *36*
   The Norns *37*
   Sol/Sunna *38*
   Nerthus *39*
   Ing *40*
   Eir *40*
   Sjöfn *40*
   Hlín *40*

Heimdallr *40*
Bragi *40*
Forseti *41*
Fulla *41*
Gefjon *41*
Gná *41*
Hödr *41*
Idhunn/Idunn *41*
Löfn *41*
Sága *42*
Snotra *42*
Syn *42*
Vali *42*
Vár *42*
Vídharr *42*
Vór *42*

The Jötnar or Etin 43
Other Supernatural Entities 43
Sacred Spaces 44
Blót and Sacrifices 45

CHAPTER 3
MODERN NORSE RELIGION AND RITUAL **49**
How Norse Religion and Rituals Survived 50
Rune Masters *51*
Folk Art and Lore: Pennsylvania Magic Staves and Art *51*
Solitary Norse Magic Workers and Worshipers *52*
Odinism and Thor Worshipers *52*
Asatrú and Northern Traditions Revival and Rediscovery *52*
Introducing Norse Magic 53
Troth *53*

CHAPTER 4
COMPLEMENTARY METHODS—SEIÐR AND SPÁ **55**
What is the Practice of Seiðr? 55
What is the Practice of Spá? 56
The Similarities of Seiðr and Spá 57

CHAPTER 5
COMPLEMENTARY METHODS—RUNES AND GALDR ..**59**
What Are Runes? 59
Similarity to Ogham *60*
What is Galdr? 61
Rune Poems and Rune Galdr *61*
More About the Staves *61*

PART II - THE RUNES

CHAPTER 6
THE FUTHARK—RUNIC ALPHABET 65
Elder and Younger Futhark 65
Correspondence in Writing 66
Note on the Elder and Younger Futhark Differences 67
Individual Rune Meanings 68
Fehu ᚠ 68
Uruz ᚢ 70
Thurisaz ᚦ 72
Ansuz ᚨ 73
Raidho ᚱ 74
Kenaz ᚲ 75
Gebo ᚷ 76
Wunjo ᚹ 77
Hagalaz ᚺ 78
Naudhiz ᚾ 79
Isa ᛁ 81
Jera ᛃ 83
Eihwaz ᛇ 84
Perthro ᛈ 85
Elhaz ᛉ 87
Sowilo ᛊ 88
Tiwaz ᛏ 90
Berkano ᛒ 92
Ehwaz ᛖ 94
Mannaz ᛗ 96
Laguz ᛚ 97
Ingwaz ᛜ 98
Dagaz ᛞ 100
Othala ᛟ 101
The Wyrd 102

CHAPTER 7
CASTING RUNES FOR DIVINATION 103
About Casting Runes for Divination 103
How Rune Reading Differs From Tarot 103
Preparation for Rune Divination 105
Making Your Own Runes vs Buying a Rune Set 105
Making Your Own Rune Set 106
Making Your Own Rune Staves 107
Purifying or Cleansing Your Runes 107
Activating or Renewing Your Runes and Rune Staves 108
Hallowing 108

Meditation or Seiðr work *109*
Invocation *109*
Methods of Rune Divination 110
The Three Norns or Past, Present, Future Cast *110*
The Grid Divination *111*
The Runic Calendar *112*
The Full Set and Circle Reading *113*
The Closing of the Divination *113*
Tips for Reading the Runes *113*

PART III - **PRACTICING MAGIC**

CHAPTER 8
PRACTICING SEIÐR 119
Soul Work or Hyge-Craft 120
    Hug 120
    Hyge 121
    Hyde 121
    Lyke 121
    Myne 121
    Wode 122
    Ond and Odr 122
    Hamingjar 122
    Godi/Gydja/Higher Self 122
About Practicing Seiðr 122
Preparation for Practicing Seiðr 123
Methods of Practicing Seiðr 124
    Wardings *124*
    Rhythmic Chants *125*
    Trance *125*
    Journeying *127*
        Calling Your Fetch 128
        Gaining More Allies and Further Journeying 130
    A Note on Possession and Riding *130*

CHAPTER 9
PRACTICING SPÁ 131
About Practicing Spá 132
Preparations for Practicing Spá 132
Methods for Practicing Spá 133
    The Light Trance *133*
    Incantations and Charms *134*
    The High Seat Ceremony *134*
    Wand Work *135*
    Runes and Omen Reading *136*

CHAPTER 10
CREATING GALDR STAVES 137
About Creating Galdr and Rune Spells 137
Preparation for Creating Galdr Staves or Taufr............................. 139
Methods for Creating Galdr Signs and Talismans 140
  Bind Runes.. 140
  Helms of Awe.. 142
  Magical Signs and Formulae.. 143
  Magical Staves 145

CONCLUSION 147

QUICK GUIDE TO RUNES 150
The Elder Futhark Quick Guide 150
The Younger Futhark Quick Guide 151
The Runic Year 152

QUICK GUIDE TO POPULAR NORSE GODS AND GODDESSES 153

GLOSSARY 157

REFERENCES 161

INTRODUCTION

You've probably seen movies with the Norse god Thor flying through the air with his hammer, chasing after his mischief-making brother Loki, golden angular inscriptions igniting whenever the two brothers wield their power. Maybe you've watched a certain TV series with Viking shieldmaidens and sinister, hooded men casting bones inscribed with those same angular symbols to forecast doom and gloom, or to predict who would next die in battle. And wouldn't you know it, the divination is almost always true, but in a dramatically twisted way the hero or heroine didn't see coming. This all makes for great entertainment, but do the Norse (Who exactly were they anyway?), their bickering gods, and their strange-seeming magic have anything to offer you in the modern world?

While much of popular culture focuses on family feuds amongst the Asgardian gods and their amazing magical artifacts, digging just a little deeper will reward you with the real-life treasure of the northern ancients who prayed to and invoked the elements, the natural world, and the supernatural world; so establishing a way to co-exist with these realms to survive harsh environments and unpredictable neighbors. This treasure was knowledge of the runes, those angular inscriptions and symbols found on almost anything Nordic. In order to recognize and appreciate this treasure of the Norse, you'll need to know and appreciate a few facts about them.

Who Were, or Are, the Norse?

The Norse originated in the Scandinavian lands of Norway, Denmark, and Sweden, and were the only people to settle in Iceland. They were mostly farmers, artisans, mariners, and merchants. The name generally translated means "Northman" or "Northerner." Some Norsemen (usually farmers) would raid lands across from them for any form of wealth, including slaves. These seasonally-marauding farmers were called "Vikings" by the English. (Kausnik, 2011. Mark, 2018.)

Over the course of the Viking Age (about c.790 to c.1100 CE) the Norse gained a reputation for their fearsome battle behavior, calling on their powerful gods for wealth and protection, and for divining the future using their "secret" alphabet—the runes. Little was understood about the runemasters, Norse diviners, priestesses, and seers who often advised on and foretold the outcome of these raids and other events.

Do People Still Practice Norse Magic and Read the Runes?

Yes! People still practice Norse magic and read runes.

Although some Norsemen converted to Christianity fairly early before the Viking Age, many resisted other religions, with Iceland narrowly averting a civil war over the question of remaining Pagan or becoming Christian. Christianity won, but the old Norse religion and myths were observed in secret and preserved in the Poetic Edda, a collection of epic and well-loved 12th-century Icelandic poems.

Throughout areas of Norse influence, the art of rune-reading, magic-working, and channeling, or "seeing," continues to be practiced, usually in secret. The tales of the Norse gods remain popular throughout the ages, with their humor and drama entertaining and preserving ancient myths.

Runes Are Hidden All Around You

Look closely and you'll see runes all around you: in advertising, on signage, and even on your smartphone and computer! Clicking on your Bluetooth often? Look again. You're clicking on a runemark—the combination of two runes. In this instance, it's the runes equivalent to 'H' ᚼ and B ᛒ, symbolic of Harald Bluetooth, a Norse warrior. Join them together and you get the sign now universally signaling 'Bluetooth' in all corners of the world. This modern sign is therefore a bind-rune—the combination of two or more runes!

Serious Stuff Only

Today we're accustomed to instant results with little thought of cost or consequences. Even with certain modern magic-working and divination, practitioners may use magic and divination energies for frivolous or inconsequential matters, and without much regard. Norse magic and rune-work demands forethought and respect for their energies and application. A price must be paid—sometimes small, sometimes large, and often unexpected. Norse magic and divination follows the practitioner only so far, for it also serves Fate and Destiny equally, and often the will of the gods, too. This can give the impression that Norse magic and rune-work is fickle. However, practitioners and those who seek an outcome may not always be aware of the greater web upon which they weave or that is perceived by them.

The wise, therefore, always keep in mind the price (often unknown) and consequences (often unseen) that may inevitably follow their work. To the Norse, this phenomenon is the "Wyrd" or "Weird." They always respect runes and magic-working, seldom using it for trivial matters.

PART I
THE NORSE

CHAPTER 1
THE NORSE IN HISTORY

The terror of British and low-lander countries in the ages before the 11th century are what comes to mind when one speaks of Norse history. Vikings, raiders, berserkers, longships, and unkempt males with merciless swords are probably the most common images you think of. But Norse history is so much richer and more complex than this popular idea.

ARE THE NORSE AND VIKINGS THE SAME PEOPLE?

Yes, the Vikings were Norse, but not all of the Norse were Viking. Like most Norse concepts, what appears on the surface is just the tip of the iceberg. Norsemen were, for the most part, farmers, merchants, craftsmen, and traders. Those that chose to go "a viking" were mostly farmers and the sons of chieftains who looked to gain more wealth and prestige during the summer when the seas were clear of ice. Other Norsemen used those same sea passages for trade and exploration.

POSSIBLE COUSINS AND ANCESTORS TO NORSE CULTURE

There's some debate about the ancestors and origins of the Norse. Most would claim their descent from Odin, but was he a god, a mighty and powerful chieftain, or an ambitious shaman? And where did Odin and his people come from if the mythology is merely a metaphor?

Linguistically, and from some origin stories, the Norse are believed to be a branch of an Indo-European tribe strongly influenced or stemming from Celts, Volsungs, Hindus, Slavs, and Balkan and Mediterranean tribes. Some also claim a Persian origin. (Anderson, 1906). It's believed that the chieftain Odin led his people on a journey north based on a divination of his that indicated their fates lay in the far north. Along the way to present day Scandinavia, Odin and his people were either conquered or were accepted and integrated into the local tribes, as Odin's magic and wisdom was said to bring bumper crops and prosperity to all of the tribes and lands he interacted with.

One tradition has Asgard situated off the Black Sea, lying by a river that then bordered Asaheim (possibly a name for the greater Asian continent). Odin's country was believed to have been separated from Tyrkland by a great mountain range (Anderson, 1906), and that Odin, his 12 priests and priestesses, his two brothers, and his people then traveled through Logrin, Russia, and onto Sigtuna, Sweden, where he eventually settled, founding the Æsir pantheon and integrating the Vanir gods, including Freya. The Norse are, therefore, kin to many of the eastern and northern tribes of the joined European and Asian continents.

The similarities don't just run linguistically, but culturally as well. Some deities are shared, or have names from the same root and function. Rituals and traditions are also echoed across the European and Asian continents, particularly in the reverence of a mother goddess, water paths, and festival days. Observances and calendars were also lunar-based, with solstices having great importance religiously and magically.

Ancient Scandinavian Culture

Horses were important and sacred animals to the Norse, some receiving their own elaborate burials. One sacred Norse ritual involved eating the meat of a sacrificed horse.

Ritual sacrificial toasts called "minni toasts" were made during some religious feasts. The host would bless the meat, then the gathering would toast Odin, followed by Njord, and then Frey. After the gods had been honored, relatives who passed away would be toasted.

In ancient Scandinavian culture the dead were buried in mounds or cremated with their possessions, much like the Egyptians and Hindus. Some mounds, like those in Gamla Uppsala, also served a ritual purpose. Cremation was introduced by the Norse to the north. "Stone ships" were burial spaces where mounds were enclosed by stone markers set out in the shape of a ship. Each person had their own mound. It's theorized that these stone ships, some with mounds built over them, symbolized the elites' journey and new home in Fólkvangr, Freya's hall in heaven, an alternative to Valhalla, Odin's hall of warriors. (Solsdottir, 2015).

Gods, especially Nerthus and Frey, and accompanied by their respective priests, toured the land in wagons, or "land ships:" wooden boats with wheels set on special wagons.

Sailing ships—longships and later merchantmen—were run by the noble and elite, with the cost falling on commoners and farmers through taxes that funded the shipbuilding and expeditions. While some believed ships represented the path of the sun's passage through the day, others said they represented the warrior spirit or inequality because of the taxes and manpower diverted to them by nobles. (Solsdottir, 2017).

It's also possible that marriage was viewed differently in ancient Scandinavian culture than by Christianity and other Western traditions. It's believed that some partnerships were open ones, portrayed in mythology by Odin and Frigg. Little stigma seemed attached to divorce as shown by the god Njord's divorce from the giantess Skadi.

The Norse believed that "orlog," or personal destiny, was not changeable, even if the Norns were petitioned. Most Norse went around with the certainty that little lasted forever. Even the warriors in Odin's hall in Valhalla would leave their feasting to fight in Ragnarok—the end of the world.

"Yggdrasil," the world tree, was central to Norse religious and creation myths, much like their Asiatic neighbors. Guarded by the Norns, the sacred tree anchors the nine worlds and allows communication between the worlds and dimensions.

Ragnarok was believed to mark the end of the world, the destruction of almost everything, including most of the Æsir and Vanir gods. From the ashes and survivors, including Yggdrasil, it was believed that life would grow again. In the new world, Modi and Magni (Thor's sons), Vali, (the god of vegetation and Odin's youngest son) and Baldur and Hodur would establish society once more. (Thorpe, et al, 1911. pp. 323-328).

THROUGH TRADE AND TERROR: AREAS OF NORSE CULTURAL INFLUENCE

When thinking of Norse expansion and cultural influence, the Viking Age is mentioned most often, despite it being relatively short, lasting from the late 700s B.C.E. to the early 1100s B.C.E.. Yet, Norse trade began long before that, from at least 300 B.C.E. (Mark, 2018).

Constant trade and extensive exploration saw Norse pioneers and adventurers reach the shores of Scotland, the Faroes, Orkney, Ireland, the Mediterranean, North America, and North Africa. They also traded on the Baltic Sea. If there was a waterway deep enough for their flat-bottomed ships to sail, they would explore it. In fact, during the Viking raids and invasion of Scotland, a ship was carried from the coast up to Loch Lomond, expanding the raider's reach inland!

The Norse had a strong trading partnership with Byzantine. They even helped with security for the Byzantine emperor, forming a special guard for him called the "Varangian Guard." But it's without doubt that their greatest influence was in the British Isles, Ireland, the North Atlantic and Arctic regions, and the Baltic region. In turn, later Norse culture was influenced by these same regions. In particular, the Finnish and Siberian shamans introduced magical and healing practices to the Norse that later produced seiðr and spá workings.

Scotland, the Faroes islands, Orkney and Ireland experienced the worst of the Viking Age, and received the most pre-Christian Norse influence. With expansive Norse settlements in these areas, Celtic and Norse cultures easily assimilated to each other to the point that it's often hard to separate their individual beliefs and practices in the British Isles, even today.

The Norse were notorious in the British Isles and Ireland for their slave-trading. These regions were the source of their "thralls" of slaves. Dublin was first established as a slave-trading center, and much of the bounty carried away from that port were healthy women, children, and young men to be used for slavery. (Pruitt, 2019).

The Norse brought "Danelaw" and their seafaring culture to the lands they invaded or settled in, except for Greenland and North America (these two regions marking their few failures at colonization). They also brought the knowledge of runes and spá-workings, as well as the worship of Odin, Frigg, Freya, and Thor. Naturally, they also influenced the local languages and folklore. Many English swear words were introduced by the Norse!

CHAPTER 2
ANCIENT NORSE RELIGION AND RITUALS

From books, photographs, and records of gatherings, we know a lot about Neo-pagan religions and rituals. These ancient religious beliefs and practices were interpreted during the 19th century revival of pre-Christian gods and led to Wicca, and other nature-focused religions, gaining popularity. As for the actual practices of the ancient Norsemen? Archeologists, anthropologists, linguists, historians, and folklorists are still piecing together evidence. Each new discovery of a howe, a longship, or a burial mound stimulates new thought and debates about the previously-sidelined roles of women, the reach of Nordic beliefs and gods, and the tools and rituals performed.

Greek, Roman, and later, Christian texts, tend to view the Norse pantheon through their patriarchal and religious lenses. They often emphasize the stories and traits that suit their own purposes. Oral tradition (where it remains), self-study, research, and remaining open to new evidence are some of the best ways to continue understanding the wyrd that the ancient Norse lived within, and that still impacts our world today.

What follows is a starting point for your studies of the Norse gods, the runes, and some magical practices. If these seem daunting at first, but if this is your true path, you'll be surprised at your growth and how your understanding of the gods and the wyrd changes as you progress through the book.

THE NORSE GODS

Should you give any credence to popular depictions in films and comics of the Norse gods? These forms of entertainment seldom pay attention to the religious significance of the gods or the rituals to honor them. That said, movies, books, and comics offer an opportunity to understand how gods adapt to our culture. However, using movie knowledge to read the runes, do rune-work, and practice seiðr is sure to only please Loki and appeal to Odin's sense of humor!

The Vanir—Frey and Njord's family—were the gods of marine and agricultural aspects, and whose rituals included sacrifices. The Æsir—Odin and his family—were the gods of war, protection, and esoteric knowledge.

Mirroring their worshippers, the Norse gods were a family of warring and impulsive farmers and merchants who often sought treasures to while away the dark winter nights or defeat their foes in every way.

Some believe these gods are legends based on chieftains and migrants from the south and east. Others argue that they are correspondences of traditional Greek and Roman gods in the Nordic lands, brought by the conquerors from the south. Still others believe Thor was the progenitor, and others believe Odin to be the same. Since much of the Norse traditions were oral, and few runic religious texts exist (that aren't influenced by Latin and Christian framing from the 10th century B.C.E onwards), you may never know if Odin is indeed the progenitor. When considering the Norse gods, it's important to view them from the lens of Norse culture. Anything else would be a disservice to them, and lead to misunderstandings for you.

It's vital to know and honor each god for your seiðr, magic, and rune-work. Some may have overlapping interests or vibes, but all have a unique energy, way of working, and way of relating to their supplicants. At the heart of your relationships and interactions with the gods there should always lie honor and respect.

Following is a short introduction to the gods. It's recommended that you read their myths and study them further in your own way and time. This will ultimately strengthen your connection and workings with them.

ODIN

Appellation: The All-father, Lord of the Wolves, The Hidden One, Gray Beard, God of Wisdom, God of War

Other names: Woden, Wodin, Grim (Hooded One), Ódhinn, Grimnir

Symbols: blackthorn staff, wolf, ravens, number nine, eagle, horse, serpent, spear, a long gray beard, a one-eyed man, a hooded man

Day of the week: Wednesday

Influences: writing, poetry, divination, rune-work, necromancy, shapeshifting, esoteric knowledge, healing, wisdom, politics

Odin is the wise man, the learned scholar, the mysterious wizard, the great strategist and manipulator. He provides knowledge, magic, and salvation; yet, you cannot trust his word or contracts for he is also a trickster god. Odin may be the ultimate serving politician, but is also self-serving. He leads, but is also deceptive. Odin, much like his brother Loki, is an instigator of chaos and change. Part of his poetic prowess lies in matchless insults.

A little known belief is that Odin has possible links to the Celtic Hooded Gods, the Genii Cucullati. This Celtic horse cult may have revered the goddess Epona. Known as the Horse Whisperers, they may have used runic magic. (Howard, 1980).

Odin drew from Earth magics associated with the Earth Mother. Both Mimer's cauldron of mead, which gave him the power of poetry, and Yggdrasil (the World Tree from which he hung to gain knowledge of the runes), are sacred to the Earth Mother in her many forms.

Known to wander the earth in disguise, Odin often appears as an elder with a long, white beard, or as a ferryman to challenge your crossing. As a ferryman, Odin sometimes guides or conducts the dead to his hall, Valhalla, or to another place in the afterlife.

There's debate whether Odin is the father, son, or rival of the oldest forms of Thor and Tiw. While Odin never wielded a hammer, nor inspired courage in warriors or upheld the laws as Tiw did, he did bring protection and prosperity to his lands, and so may have displaced Thor and Tiw as the chief god when the noble class grew.

Odin was most popular with the nobles, poets, and magic-workers, so more knowledge has been preserved about him than most of the other gods. Every nine years, great blóts (ceremonies) were held for him, and often involved various forms of ritual sacrifice. With Odin's strong link to sacrificial rituals and metaphor, there's a growing debate whether his calls for sacrifice were metaphorical and self-sacrificial, or if the animal and human sacrifices were actually practiced by adherents.

Odin is often likened to the Roman god Mercury. They both rule communication, travel, trickery, invention, and problem-solving.

Odin's special rune is <u>Ansuz</u> ᚨ or 'Os' or 'Ás.'

FRIGG

Appellation: The All-Mother

Other names: Frigga, Frea

Symbols: torc, bracelets, long hair, sows, falcons, ospreys

Day of the week: Friday

Influences: fertility, good health, magical cycles, love, sovereignty, spinning and weaving, domesticity, motherhood, marriage

Frigg, or Frigga—wife of Odin and mother of Baldur—is believed to be an Earth Mother, and possibly an aspect of Nerthus. Frigg is the goddess of birth and housewives. She embodies the "perfect wife," taking care of all household and hosting duties while mothering those around her. She is the respectable courtly regent, surrounded by her entourage of helpers. A spinner of thread, she has links to the Norns who dispense fate and destiny to all—even the gods. She holds great influence and isn't afraid to wield it for causes she believes in, as well as for her supplicants that she deems worthy. While she doesn't often challenge Odin, when she does she tends to get the better of him.

Frigg is also the goddess of love, seeing to a wider sense of love rather than just the physical: affection, mother-love, self-love, and greater love and care for the community and environment.

A blood relation to Thor, Frigg has strong family connections to the land and agriculture. Her many facets and areas of rule are expressed in her "handmaidens" who carry aspects of healing, love, protection, and more.

As she was the only other person allowed to sit on the throne of Asgard, her relationship with Odin's brothers Vili and Ve granted them sovereignty, thus maintaining stability of the Æsir until Odin's return.

Her runes may be Berkano or Gebo and she is likened to the Roman goddess Venus.

Frigg overlaps with Freya, as well as The Norns. Her spinning supplies the thread that the Norns use to bestow orlog (destiny or fate) on a person.

In her healer aspect, she is, or sends, Eir the healer goddess.

FREYA

Appellation: The Lady, The Giver, The Goddess of Love and Beauty

Other names: Freia, Freyja, Syr, Sea-Bright

Symbols: black cats, a chariot drawn by black cats, sows, falcons

Day of the week: Monday

Influences: prophecy, shape-shifting, astral travel, sacrifices, battle, reaping those fallen in battle, intuition, fertility

Freya was believed to be the first priestess to preside over a sacrifice, and was the one who introduced this practice to the followers of Odin. Freya is the seeress and prophetess, and so is the patron of the seeresses or priestesses called "völvur" who foresee events and matters concerning such aspects as crops and voyage outcomes.

Freya led the Valkyries to retrieve half of all fallen warriors, taking them to Folkvangr—an alternative hall to Valhalla—where the fallen warriors lived a good afterlife.

While Odin used runes and rune-work, Freya's magic takes the form of seiðr—a trance— to conduct magic. Her planet or astronomical symbol is the moon.

Freya and Frigga often overlap and may have stemmed from the Earth Goddess, albeit from different traditions (Vanir and Æsir).

Tiw

Appellation: God of Law, God of Courage, God of War and Peace, Spirit Warrior, One-Handed, Feeder of Wolves

Other names: Tyr, Tiu, Ziu, Tig

Symbols: oath rings

Day of the week: Tuesday

Influences: law, measurement, justice, trust, logic, thought, service to family and community, pragmatism, negotiation, contracts, guarantors, victory, war, peace

Tiw is the warrior, the arbitrator, the most valiant and trustworthy of the gods. Mysterious Tiw is a sky-god, and a moderator at "things" (public assemblies) as well as at other legal and social gatherings where contracts and justice are discussed. Tiw was also the god of not just war, but also peace. Warriors called on Tiw and carved his rune, Tiwaz, on their weapons for courage and victory in battle, or for justice while going through legal issues.

Tyr is intelligent as well as valiant. He was the only god to step forward to offer surety to Fenrir the wolf when the Æsir tried to bind the menace to their society. He chose to do so knowing Odin's word was not to be trusted, and that he was almost certain to lose his arm. Some see this as an echo of Odin winning a battle for supremacy with Tiw.

Tiw is likened to Mars with his warrior and arbitrator energy. As his name is also used as a way to say "god," it's often used in kennings (allusions) of Odin and Thor. Some believe he was an aspect of one or the other, or both. Tiw, or Tyr, is often listed in the gatherings of the Æsir. Many believe his role in Asgard was larger than currently known, and that he might have been a "pre-Odin," or was displaced by Odin at some early point of the Æsir's expansion. Nevertheless, Tiw's name and presence has persisted through the years, signaling his importance or popularity, or maybe even both.

THOR

Appellation: The Thunder God, The Thunderer

Other names: Thunar, Thorr, Tror

Symbols: hammer, thunderbolt, goat, lightning, belt, iron gloves

Day of the week: Thursday

Influences: avenging, agriculture, courage in battle, defending, strength, the weather, blessings

Thor is like a strong anchor or anvil you can lean on, grounding and protecting energy. Thor is the avenger who seeks out threats and destroys them. He's the straight-forward, uncomplicated, no-frills "jarl," (chief) who calls things as he sees them. He's also the bad-tempered relative who'll smite any annoyance with little thought. He may be underestimated and be confused at times, but despite his temper, it's hard not to love him.

Despite this infamous temper, Thor was entrusted with one of the most powerful weapons in the land; a weapon that even Odin could not wield: the hammer "Mjölnir."

Thor is often likened to Jupiter and has remained a popular god through the ages, often enjoying more popularity than even Odin. Thor is also likened to a bad-tempered, simple Hercules. His popularity often defied Christian edicts when people continued to carve his rune and invoke his blessings and protection.

Thor was most popular with farmers and thralls (slaves), likely one of the reasons the other more courtly gods made fun of his apppearance and straight-forwardness; yet, they depended on him to safe-keep their home from the "Jötnar" (giants).

As an ancient weather god, Thor saw to healthy crops, blessed blóts, and hallowed with hammer and anvil. Occasionally, he was invoked in healing rituals, and to end plagues. Some say Thor may sit as a judge at the foot of Yggdrasil at certain times near Ragnarok. Generally, Thor looks to fulfill most of the roles of a good jarl.

Ullr

Appellation: Ullr, God of Winter and Snow, The Hunter God, God with the Skis, God with the Shield, God of Combat

Other names: Ullr, Ullinn, Ullern (possibly Ollerus and Wuldor)

Symbols: skis, bow, shield

Influences: hunting, sports, pragmatism, winter, protection, combat, safe-keeping

Ullr is the God of Winter, the hunter, and the patron of snow and snow activities ,from skiing and snowboarding to ice-skating. To the Norse, "Ullr's ship" was a kenning for a shield. Ullr travels on skis and hunts with his bow.

Invoked in oaths using metal rings, Ullr was even invoked by Odin when the All-Father was in a bind, listing Ullr first when a battle was planned. Some go even further and claim that Ullr led and protected the Æsir when Odin was traveling or wandering.

Some believe he is an aspect of Tiw, as they were both warriors, and oaths in which they were invoked were binding.

Frey

Appellation: Lord of Prosperity, God of the World, God of Plenty, The Fruitful Lord

Other names: Freyr

Symbols: horse, boar, deer/stag, a chariot pulled by a boar, a golden boar

Influences: peace, material things, physical passion, physical health, the land, the airspace over the land, sacrifices, fertility

Frey—Freyr—is the bringer of fertility and vitality to crops and his people. He is the sustainer of prosperity and peace, and the lover who would risk all for his beloved's heart.

Associated with or also known as Ing or Yngvi, Frey blessed the land by plowing it once a year. Like his father Njord, he was also the god who blessed the seas and ships.

Although primarily a peace-maker, Frey was also respected for his warrior status, having, along with the other Vanir, fought the Æsir into a stalemate when they sought to invade.

Frey was associated with elves, and may have been their ruler in Alfheim.

BALDUR

Appellation: God of Summer, God of the Sun, God of Spring

Other names: Baldr, Balder

Symbols: mistletoe

Day of the week: Sunday

Influences: eloquence, beauty, healing, resurrection, self-confidence, premonition, popularity

Baldur, son of Frigg and Odin, brother to Hödr, is the shining star of the Norse. He's friendly, approachable, and beloved by all. Baldur is neither a winner nor a loser when it comes to fate. His death is said to provoke Ragnarok, and Ragnarok making it possible for his return to the land of the living when he'll rule along with others.

Together with his wife, Nanna, he helped his family in Asgard to find a sanctuary of peace and healing at his home.

The astronomical object associated with Baldur is the sun.

Loki

Appellation: The Trickster, The Shape Changer, Father of Monsters

Other names: Lokki

Symbols: Double-horned helmet, mistletoe, entwined serpents

Influences: cunning, beauty, deception, humor, shadow-side, change, interference, illusion, destruction

Loki is the blood-brother of Odin, helping the Asgardians at first, but never being accepted by them. Loki is the trickster, leaving some laughing, and others crying. A master of disguise and cunning, Loki is the one whose illusions last the longest. He, along with Thor, was the one who Odin called to solve the most embarrassing and delicate of Asgardian problems. Loki was often winning through guile and intelligence.

Loki speaks to the shadow-side, the malicious side, the deceptive side—the ego that cannot be denied nor leave an insult unanswered.

Loki is associated with the element of air.

A master at "flything" (trading insults), Loki's mouth was known to cause him immense trouble.

Through his mischief-making and humor-driven actions, it's often said that Loki is the tool of change for the Norse while Odin is its instigator. By creating the greatest destruction of the old order, Loki's actions aid the workings of destiny to bring about Ragnarok and welcome the new age.

NJORD

Appellation: The Wealthy, The Ruler of Men, God of the Seafarers

Other names: Njorth, Njördhr, Niord

Symbols: ships, metal objects

Influences: abundance, prosperity, the sea, the airspace above seas and oceans, peace, incompatibility

Njord is the successful, benevolent king who values peace but is not afraid to go to war. He's the patron of sailors, merchants, and warriors. Under his rule, his lands saw a golden period of prosperity, long lives, and few illnesses. Njord is the diplomat willing to sacrifice his own happiness in order to cease hostilities and bring peace and wellbeing to his people. Unlucky in love, Njord doesn't hold grudges.

One of the Vanirs who held the Æsir to a stalemate before integrating with them, Njord is the father of Freya and Frey, his first wife being Nerthus, the Earth Mother. He, too, was a very popular god and was widely worshiped.

Njord was seen as the Neptune or Saturn of the Norse world, although he was not the God of the Seas. His ability to rule wisely and to the benefit of his people ensure he was held in high regard.

He may have been supplanted by Odin as the most influential and popular god, but he and his son, Frey, were still honored after Odin in toasts and other rituals.

THE NORNS

Appellation: The Fates

Other names: The Triple Goddess

Symbols: the wyrd rune, the loom, thread

Day of the week: Saturday

Influences: destiny, fate

The Norns are the three sisters who dispense destinies, remaining detached no matter the results of fate. They are the three who tend the World Tree, Yggdrasil, protecting it from harm. The Norns are the runemasters who may have known the powerful letters before they were perceived by Odin. The sisters didn't need to demand respect, they got it anyway.

These three sisters preside over the fate of both mortals and gods, giving the individuals their "orlog." But while they set destinies in motion, they make no changes to the work they've done. The Fates send out other lesser Norns who carry the "orlog" of newborns to them. Other Norns were also sent by the elves and dwarfs to mortals.

Working within the wyrd, the Norns weave people's destinies, and seldom share their knowledge of fate.

The sisters are invoked by rune-workers as Past (Urd or Weird), Present (Verdandi), and Future (Skuld). They may have also carved twigs/staves, using rune magic to protect Yggdrasil and its environment. (Solsdottir, 2017).

As part of their duties, the Norns guard the "Well of Urd," also known as the "Well of Wyrd," that provides water for Yggdrasil. They also nourish the World Tree with mead.

The sisters are associated with the Triple Goddess in her forms of maiden, mother, and crone. Their rune may be Neid or Naudhiz. They share Saturn and Saturday with Njord.

Sol/Sunna

Appellation: Mistress of the Sun, Bright Bride

Other names: Fairwheel, All Bright, Everglow, Gull, Elfin Beam

Symbols: golden chariot, horses, gold and yellow items, stone

Day of the week: Sunday

Influences: blessings, travel, cycles, healing, renewal, rebirth, continuity

Sol (or Sunna) is the bright and beautiful goddess who rides the life-giving sun across the sky on a chariot drawn by two horses. She's the terror of the dwarves (who live in the dark or underground) with her illumination. With her sisters, Sol sings healing incantations, and through her future daughter who may also be called Sol, she'll ensure the continuity of the life-giving sun after Ragnarok.

At night, much like Osiris, she may journey through the underworld before once again resuming her chariot race across the sky, chased by the wolf, Skoll, who will devour her during Ragnarok (but before that, her daughter will be born).

Sol is related to the álfar—the elves or Light Elves of Alfheim—ruled by Freyr. Her rune is Sowilo ᛋ.

NERTHUS

Appellation: Earth Mother, Great Earth Mother

Other names: Unknown

Symbols: cart, landships

Influences: fertility, peace, purity, secrecy

Nerthus is mysterious. She's the Earth Mother related to the Berkano rune, regarded by some as the Great Earth Mother. She gives life and she takes life. She's the bringer of peace and plenty, but maybe at the cost of terror. As the Earth Mother, she holds great powers over all aspects of human life.

Little is known about Nerthus, and those accounts are often debated. Nerthus is believed to have been an unseen goddess who toured her lands in a landship, a ship with four wheels that looks like a cart drawn by two cows.

Iron and the pursuit of war or violence was not allowed in her presence, only revelry and peace, and only her priest was allowed to touch her cart.

After her tour, she (or rather her earthly possessions) were cleansed in a mysterious lake. Slaves who'd helped clean the cart and the goddess were drowned.

In another account, she is Njord's sister, or wife, or both, and was killed by the Æsir in the great war that no one won.

ING

Other names: Yngvi

Symbols: cart, landship

Influence: fertility

Ing is believed to be the ancient corn god who preceded Frey. Their attributes and roles are therefore quite similar. Ing is the consort of Nerthus.

Ingwaz ◊ is his rune.

EIR

One of Frigg's handmaidens, or an aspect of Frigg, Eir is the healer goddess. She is also the physician to the gods.

SJÖFN

A handmaiden of Frigg, Sjofn is the Goddess of Love and Affection. She helps in all matters of the emotional heart.

HLÍN

The fiercest of Friggs' handmaidens, Hlin is the Goddess of Protection, especially physical protection.

HEIMDALLR

The guardian of Bifrost and protector of Asgard, Heimdallr can perceive far and wide across the universe. He's also the patron of clairvoyants and those whose vigilance guards and protects.

BRAGI

Husband to Idunn and poet to the gods, Bragi is the God of Eloquence, overseeing good communication, be it verbal or written.

Forseti

The God of Reconciliation and Justice, Forseti can bring harmony to opposing sides through resolving differences.

Fulla

The first handmaiden of Frigg, Fulla is the goddess' personal assistant, helping Frigg have greater impact. She's the ultimate helper.

Gefjon

Believed to be an aspect of Freya, Gefjon is the Goddess of Gifts and Virtue. She brings gifts of beauty, spirit, the material, and grace to a situation.

Gná

An aspect of Frigg, or one of her handmaidens, Gná is the Goddess of Transformation, helping in self-growth and perception.

Hödr

A son of Odin, Hödr embodies conflict and is the God of Blind Force. He helps you find brute strength and force.

Idhunn/Idunn

The guardian of the golden apples of youth, Idhunn is the Goddess of Renewal and Regeneration. She ensures the vital force of energy and life remains high in all beings.

Löfn

Aspects of Frigg and Odin, Löfn is the Goddess of Indulgence who grants permission for things and actions that are lawfully forbidden.

SÁGA

An aspect of Frigg also called the Seeress, Sága prophesizes and has great knowledge of the wyrd.

SNOTRA

A handmaiden of Frigg, Snotra is the Goddess of Intelligence.

SYN

The lawyer of the gods, The Goddess of Denial is the defender of the accused. She also provides legal help.

VALI

One of Odin's sons, Vali is the God of Vengeance. He avenged his brother Baldur and will survive Ragnarok to help establish a new world.

VÁR

The Goddess of Truth and Honesty, she ensures contracts broken, including promises and vows, are suitably punished. She may be an aspect or helper of Njord and Tiw.

VÍDHARR

The God Silence and Vengeance, Vídharr helps in dealing with crises.

VÓR

The Goddess of Awareness, like Heimdallr, is aware of everything and everyone. She sees the truth and can perceive what is hidden.

The Jötnar or Etin

The third tribe of gods or god-like beings, the Jötnar (Jötunn singular, also called Etins) are the elemental beings—the giants whom the Æsir fought and held at bay. Strangely, the Jötnar are kin to many of the Æsir and are still sought out by Odin, their half-brother, when his knowledge and wisdom fail him.

The Jötnar, who play a significant role in Norse lore, are: Loki, Hela, Mimir, Sif, Skadi, Angrboda, Sigyn, Fenris, Jord, Jordmundgard, Surt, and Vali.

Unlike the Vanir, and despite the strong family ties, the Jötnar have never been integrated into the Æsir tribe or vice versa. It's a toxic tie between the two tribes.

The Jötnar are regarded as the elemental and shadow side to the Norse religion. They represent the aspects of nature that cannot be controlled or even predicted: the ice, the fire, the waters, and the land. They, too, are a part of the wyrd, and their threads are woven in with the Æsir. Through chaos and upheaval they bring change. While they might often be destructive and malevolent, their wisdom just as often saves the world from calamity.

Strangely, too, the Jötnar held some of the most sought after treasures that the Æsir had to steal. There's a debate among those who honor the Jötnar as well as the Æsir and Vanir, and those who demonize them. How you view them lies with you, and your view will determine your path through the Norse traditions.

While the debate rages whether Jötnar should also be venerated, a growing number of heathens believe honoring the Jötnar for their positive contributions to life and survival, and learning about the shadow side with their help, is a good thing.

Other Supernatural Entities

Fetch: An energetic analog of yourself or a guide of yours in the astral plane. Your fetch can be your mirrored self, your fetch-husband, fetch-wife, fetch-deer (any animal), or an abstract shape. Often your fetch animal is your totem animal.

Wight: Any being with life-force running through them. These can be humanoids or from the natural world, or even created by a strong magic-worker.

Dís or Díses: Ancestral female spirits who can be called on to help in the astral plane. They are also present at childbirth.

SACRED SPACES

The Norse worshiped and practiced magic outdoors. Later, with the influence of southern practices and Christianity, they built wooden temples or churches.

Sacred space or ground can either be found in nature or claimed through ritual.

Places of great natural beauty, of geological significance, or where the veil is thin between worlds are often innately sacred and immediately identifiable by any person. These naturally-sanctified spots are often very powerful locations for earth and other magic.

Outdoors or within a temple, sacred spaces are consecrated, or hallowed (set free of negative energies or malevolent beings), allowing for worship and magic work without uninvited interference. These spaces are then reserved only for worship or magic work.

Fortunately, there are easy ways to hallow land:

- Fire is one of the best known ways to hallow. Setting bonfires or torches at various points to enclose a space has long been practiced. This is often followed by a verbal declaration of consecration.

- Invoking Thor/Thunor. The Thunder God's protection is usually enough to hallow ground. Mark a boundary and, using a pendant or other talisman, or carving the Thorn rune at different points, ask Thor to hallow the ground. Alternatively, make a hammer sign with your hand and fist and invoke Thor to make the area sacred.

- Carry soil or a relic from another holy or sacred site and sprinkle it or use amounts of it to demarcate the sacred area.
- Placing symbols at various points of the area can also hallow the ground.
- Hazel rods or pillars can also be used to hallow ground. Ring the area with hazel rods and link them with rope so you have a hazel and rope fence. Call on Thor to complete the hallowing.

Trees and their environments can also be sacred spaces. Yggdrasil is one such case. Ash and yew are more likely candidates as a focus for a sacred space as both trees have powerful protective energies and are sacred in themselves.

Groves, especially those with waterfalls, are also innately sacred or easily hallowed for worship and magic. Volva would often prophecy in groves and temples that were later situated in those ancient sacred spaces. Ancient sacred groves usually have rocks or other markers carved with thanks to the gods, or the symbol of the god who was most worshiped in that space.

Hallowed ground was called "vier" or "vi" and could also refer to a shrine.

Blót and Sacrifices

Blóts are rituals of worship that mark key points of lives and the Norse year. They are done at weddings and funerals, at solstices and festivals, and for specific gods in honor or to ask for favor. Blóts are also done to honor the dead, the valorous, and to honor the community. At large events, blóts are also done to open and close the proceedings.

These ceremonies were hosted in sacred spaces and temples or dedicated structures called "hofs." They were also conducted at "haughrs," or mounds or barrows. Frey's mound at Uppsala was one of the most famous mounds where blóts were regularly held.

Great blóts were hosted by, and officiated by, the nobles and wealthy on their lands. During these ceremonies, the host was the Gode (the priest). By providing food and drink to the community gathered for the celebrations, blóts also underlined that the magnate hosting the ceremony had social standing and the blessing of their god. In smaller groups, blóts were also performed during religious and cultural gatherings. Community was a large focus of these great ceremonies, with attendees feasting together on the blessed offerings.

Sacrifices and "a god's share," or libations, are usually part of a blót. Food and drink, mostly mead, were commonly offered. Objects of personal or monetary value to a devotee were offered to the god in exchange for protection or favor. Tyr, the God of War and Peace, received offerings of weapons, while Freya received offerings of jewelry. Offerings were viewed more as gifts to the gods, with the expectation that a gift of equal or greater value would be returned.

Animal sacrifices, including horses, were made by the priestesses, the wealthy, and the rulers, but not very often by the farmers and thralls. Occasionally, humans were sacrificed to Odin. Blood was collected in bowls, and a twig or spray of leaves was then dipped into the blood and was sprinkled across the worshipers and sacred area. Any blood left in the bowl once this was done was poured back to the earth or returned to the god via a receptacle with thanks and blessings. In non-blood sacrifices, the same was done with mead or other offered liquids.

When animals were slaughtered, the gathered fed on the meat and drank mead or ale—feasting on the blessings of the god. Boasts, or toasts, were made to Odin, Njord, and Frey, as well as to the god being honored, ancestors, and valorous warriors. "A good harvest" or "surviving the winter" were requests made to these gods.

Not every sacrifice involved slaughter. Hanging from a sacred tree in a grove, or placing the sacrificed in a well were also ancient methods of sacrifice, depending on the god whose favor was sought. Fortunately, these practices were discontinued in time as other methods of sacrifice and blood for ritual use became acceptable.

Blóts can be as small or big as you wish. They can also be elaborate or very simple, depending on your and the god's preferences.

CHAPTER 3
MODERN NORSE RELIGION AND RITUAL

For many of the modern followers of the Old Ways and gods, their religion and perceived beliefs can be upsetting and a great point of contention with those around them. Since the misappropriation of signs, symbols, and gods by the 19th century German Romantic Movement, those that follow the traditions and gods of the Norse religion have been lumped in with groups and political movements who often don't hold with or understand the fundamentals of the old religion and its rituals.

The most notoriously misappropriated sign was Sunna's sign of the Sun Wheel or Wheel of Life, used by the Nazis, and commonly known as the "swastika." This sign is also precious to the Hindu goddess, Shakti.

Since World War 2, Norse, pagan, and other communities have viewed these perversions of their religious and cultural symbols with concern, and have fought to distance themselves from groups who promote and practice racism and other forms for discrimination that run counter to the tenets of Norse religion. They also work to claim back their symbols of power and balanced cohesion with the natural and supernatural world.

Recently, Asatrú followers and neo-pagans of every color and creed have been distancing their organizations from racist and others haters, and are actively working to ensure the Norse religion and its practices remain free and open to everyone and anyone who feels called to this path. Declaration 127 follows Odin's words from the Hávamál that states, "When you see misdeeds, speak out against them, and give your enemies no peace."

Fortunately, as the need to return to earth-based religions and to honor all aspects of self and the divine grow, the tarnish is wearing off Norse religions and beliefs. People are starting to understand them better and see similarities with other beliefs and religions around the world.

How Norse Religion and Rituals Survived

When Christianity started to become dominant in Scandinavia, the Norse gods and their followers co-existed, influencing each other. The magic of the vitkar and völvur also began to change in some regions, adopting some of the Latin words and forms, but still invoking the Norse gods.

Soon, the new Christian religion became dominant, and old religion and magics were outlawed in all of Scandinavia except Iceland. The oral traditions were lost to the mainlanders with their Christian rituals colored by their former rites and observances. All vitkar, völvur, and seiðr workers were branded evil and sorcerous. Only the spaewives of Orkney and a few other spá workers were tolerated. All other seiðr and spá work was branded witchcraft. Still, the practices were followed as best they could in secret.

During the early 10th century C.E, Iceland was split almost 50-50 between those Norse who wished to continue their old religion and those who wished all to be Christians. Christianity prevailed, but unlike other Scandinavian countries, the Norse religion was allowed a short respite before it was outlawed. Scholars used this time to write the Eddas and preserve as much of the knowledge and rituals of the Norse gods as they could. Then, in a uniquely Icelandic way, the Old Religion was tolerated—but only if it was practiced in secret. Our knowledge of the last days of the Norse religion being widely and openly practiced therefore comes from Icelandic sources (and a few other earlier Latin and Greek sources.) Using this knowledge, modern practices of the Northern Tradition and Asatrú—the name given to the Norse religion—was reconstructed, and through practice, rediscovered.

RUNE MASTERS

Rune-work and knowledge were marginally retained while the Norse religion was outlawed. In Iceland, the use of bind runes with the names of the Norse gods and magic charms were hidden in decorative art. Curved lines were introduced, and these Norse talismans flourished, carved in wood and metal. Called Galdrastafur, or magic staves, they gradually became formulaic and were collected in books like the Galdrabók, a grimoire compiled in the 17th century. Throughout, the runes were known as mystical secret writing, and got a reputation for presenting users with dire and evil repercussions. Because of this, most folk avoided their use, and the reading of runes and mundane rune messages died out. However, spaewives and spae-men retained some knowledge of the runes when they sang galdr and ristered magical signs, otherwise known as runes in the air.

FOLK ART AND LORE: PENNSYLVANIA MAGIC STAVES AND ART

Runes and the heroic tales of warrior and magic-working Æsir and Vanir gods persisted in folklore and folk art. Knowledge of the Jötnar remained as trolls and giants in fairy tales, cautionary tales, and horror stories. Meanwhile, the dwarves and the alfs became bedtime stories for young ones, and cautionary tales for young adults who might turn away from their prescribed religion. And, in an odd twist worthy of a skald's poem, the New World became home to the old lore and magical signs.

The Pennsylvania Dutch hex signs, their farming, witchcraft, superstitions, and their habit of consulting wise women like Mountain Mary—die Berg Maria—all stem from the old Norse and Germanic religions of their forefathers. These practices survived unchanged for over 200 years. (Thorsson, 1993). Like the seiðr workers of old, each sign maker or hex-master taught their craft to one or two others in the community. Fortunately, some of this lore and technique has been recorded, preserving the American contribution to the ancient Nordic and Germanic art of casting magical signs.

SOLITARY NORSE MAGIC WORKERS AND WORSHIPERS

Then we have the wild men and women of the forests and isolated places practicing their magic and honoring the Norse gods and Jötnar away from persecution. While they may have lost the ceremony of the community spá divinations and long festivals to honor Odin every nine years, they retained and practiced enough of the lore that we can still deduce and observe some of the ancient rites that may have begun before Odin hung on Yggdrasil. We called these wild seiðr workers "shaman" and "witches," consulting them in secret when the prescribed ways didn't work.

ODINISM AND THOR WORSHIPERS

Thor's hammer could not be bent, broken, nor wielded by other gods and religions, and he remained popular throughout Scandinavia. Gretna Green married runaway lovers over an anvil consecrated to him, while farmers made the sign of Mjolnir in their crofts and open fields to protect their lambs and cattle.

Odinism, the worship of the All Father, persisted as well, though not as openly. Secret societies, in much the same way as the secret Asatrú temples, persevered and followed the Odinic initiation rites to empower their members and gain his wisdom and favor.

ASATRÚ AND NORTHERN TRADITIONS REVIVAL AND REDISCOVERY

In 1973, after more than 970 years, Iceland began formally recognizing Asatrú as a religion. In 1993, the Danish Asatró church was formally recognized. Though initially having only a few congregants, these temples are gaining members each year, and allowing their faith to be explored by the curious and those drawn to it. Meanwhile, more and more people are discovering the Northern Traditions and Norse religion. Some study it out of interest and as a layover on their long spiritual journey, while others are called true (meaning loyal or faithful) believers. And with each person rediscovering Norse magic and religion, the gods and the way of the wyrd is becoming more and more clear to those who wish to seek their knowledge.

INTRODUCING NORSE MAGIC

Norse magic draws on aspects of ritual magic from across the European and Asian continents. With its roots in shared shamanistic practices, and reverence for the Earth Mother and cosmic cycles, Norse magic isn't entirely unfamiliar to students of the esoteric, but it does have rules and precepts that are stricter than others.

"A gift demands a gift" is one of the most important tenets of Norse magic. (Howard, 1980). Blóts are used to gift a god with the understanding that answers to prayers would be the gift in exchange, but to ask for more than a fair exchange is to invite a greater price to pay at a later stage. An energy-worker, witch, or wizard, would describe the process as a fair exchange of energy.

TROTH

Troth is another foundation stone of Norse culture and magic practice. Meaning faith or loyalty, troth ensured that one's word or promise was binding. The word "betrothed" comes from the swearing of an oath to marry another. Similarly, to give your troth to your god, leader, or community bonded you to your promise to them for life. To swear a troth is therefore not an action to be taken lightly. Breaking troth often leads to anger, and worse, from the gods and those who considered themselves betrayed. Today the troth is another way of saying Asatrú.

While Norse magic is generally neutral in itself as is all magic—except for the curse runes—the application of any magic for "good" or "evil" and the resulting consequences rest on the magic-worker. The universal magical law in which your impact is returned 3 times 3 to you applies to Norse magic, too. (Howard, 1980). This is another reason to consider your motivations, as well as the most dire consequences possible, before attempting retaliatory or harmful magical work.

Norse magic-workers—sorcerers, magicians, soothsayers and wise men and women—are called vitki. Some prefer to work in communities, others prefer to practice alone.

Four types of Norse magic are practiced most often: seiðr, spá, rune casting, and galdr.

CHAPTER 4
COMPLEMENTARY METHODS—SEIÐR AND SPÁ

Seiðr and spá don't usually require rune-work. Practiced by the highly regarded priestesses called völvurs, spá was primarily used for predictions and prophecy, astral travel to gain information, and to contact the spirits and gods. Greek and Roman chroniclers usually refer to these practitioners as "sybils" or "prophetesses." Seiðr was concerned with manipulating aspects of a soul—for good or for bad—and was traditionally thought of as a "woman's magic." While some men did practice seiðr and spá, they weren't given the same respect as the völvurs. Fortunately, modern Norse magic-workers are more accepting of seiðr and spá workers of all genders and inclinations.

WHAT IS THE PRACTICE OF SEIÐR?

Seiðr is inner work done to receive messages and information about the outer world or other realms. It's a shamanistic form of magic that some say was taught to Odin by Freya. Also known as seith or seidh, it requires reaching a trance state to interact and interpret the wyrd and other dimensions. It also engages with allies and enemies, or other targeted folk, on a soul level on the astral planes. Seiðr practitioners can astral travel, interact with the spirit and godly realms, and shape-shift in their quests for knowledge and solutions. They were also called upon to produce illusions or other manipulation of the enemy's mind during battles.

To reach a suitable trance state when required, initiates use entheogens (natural psychedelic substances) and are trained in physical methods to reach a deep altered state of consciousness, including sexual and ecstatic practices that are similar to tantric sex. Music and rhythm are also keys to achieving the trance, with völvurs singing or chanting while playing a hide drum in sacred groves and spaces in preparation for astral travel or prophesying.

Seiðr is closely linked to modern Wicca and to the Vanir gods, in particular Freya and Frey. Utilizing curses as well as cures, practitioners were most frequently on the fringes of society, not trusted by most folk as they could easily do silent harm as well as good. This was the form of magic most vilified and persecuted by the Christian churches, often demonizing seiðr and labeling its practitioners as evil witches and sorcerers.

Today seiðr and similar practices form the initiatory process for rune-masters and other vitkar (magicians, sorcerers, or wizards) takes three years or more to complete, yet it was also the magic form practiced by the common folk in their farms, too.

It's important to note that while seiðr shares much in common with Northern shamanistic practices by the Sámi and Inuit, it's argued that it's not truly a shamanistic practice. (Gunnarsson, n.d.).

What is the Practice of Spá?

Also called spae in Scotland, Orkney, and England, spá is the reading of a person's fate or orlog as dispensed by the Norns by using intuition or divine knowledge. Practitioners were called spákona or spaewives. Spá workers would be considered the soothsayers, the fortune tellers, the wise women who used charms of voice and domestic ritual to heal, control the weather (if only temporarily), to influence those around them, and to give advice on agricultural, domestic, and love problems. Spá workers were often healers and galdr workers, too, playing an important role of serving the community and keeping it healthy and safe.

Goddesses were believed to have practiced spá—Odin, too. (Ward, n.d.). Frigg and Sif, Thor's wives—were both believed to have known the orlog of everyone along with Odin.

Völvurs, known as prophetesses, were also called spákona. Using chants and sacrifice to aid their intuition and will, spákonas occasionally use runes, too.

THE SIMILARITIES OF SEIÐR AND SPÁ

Both seiðr and spá were considered "woman's magic," and practitioners of both shared the same level of persecution as witches during the witch trials, and even later.

While seiðr and spá workers do sometimes use runes for divination and wardings, they tend not to depend on runes and runic lore to divine or weave a new event into time. Instead, they rely on their inner knowledge, their intuition, and on their perception of the domestic and natural environment around them. They may use tea-leaves or dried herbs to tell a fortune, conduct a healing through force of will and a healing charm, or fashion a protective charm from the weaving of energy over flour or ash, or even wood and spit. This form of magic was of the common folk: the farmers, the fisherman, the crafts people, and the smiths. Women, and the few men who dedicated their lives to seiðr and spá practices, were usually of the community but not in it, because seiðr and spá were also thought of as tools to create deception and manipulation to control members of the community.

If a person suspected or showed signs of being influenced by or suffering from delusions caused by seiðr, a spaekona may have been called in to counter and break the hold of the seiðr's spell on a person. Fairy tales such as Katherine Crackernuts and East of the Sun, West of the Moon echo such breaking of seiðr spells and curses.

Both seiðr and spá workers, once fully initiated and proficient enough to serve others with their magic, wore special regalia. A blue mantle or hooded cloak signified they were vitkar or völvur. Rune-masters would also wear such cloaks, as the color was special to Odin. Belts, to which a pouch filled with herbs and talismans was attached, was another mark of a magic worker. A head-dress of skins, and the use of feathers on the cloak or elsewhere, was another badge of office.

It takes equally long to master seiðr and spá. The skill and maturity needed to control the energies, then to create magic with them, takes years to master.

CHAPTER 5
COMPLEMENTARY METHODS— RUNES AND GALDR

Runes and galdr are probably what first comes to mind when someone says "Norse Magic." The mysterious symbols and the incantations of great power by a hooded figure have been familiar tropes in popular culture through fairy tales, fantasy books, and many genres of movies.

Rune divination requires no foreknowledge of galdr, while galdr requires some knowledge of rune poems and incantations. Galdr increases the potency of other forms of runic magic, but can also be used as a spell by itself.

What Are Runes?

Runes are Northern hieroglyphs, the magic writing found across much of Europe and Asia. Their forms are angular, making them easier to inscribe or carve on stone, wood, and bone. They are drawn in the air and in the soil, too. Rune staves—runes carved or burned on twigs and small branches—were commonly used for a variety of purposes.

Runes carry, or can be described as portals to, the ancient and primal forces that still influence our lives: the elements of our world, the emotions of our hearts, and the mysteries of the wyrd. These primordial energies are what make runes and their magic so dynamic and potent.

Prior to the 12th century C.E, runes were used solely for religious, magic, and legal purposes, their power binding and strong. As the need for a true alphabet arose, runes were the natural choice, updated with new letters and read much as English is. With the Old Ways challenged by Christianity, knowledge starting to be concealed or lost, and the runic alphabet incorporating the magical runes, more people used them for everyday and mundane purposes. In fact, in Orkney and other places, Viking graffiti to the effect of "'Ottarfila carved these runes" appears on ancient monuments. (Towrie, n.d-e).

Yet, runes persist in their power and potency when used in prescribed ways of the trained and talented rune-workers. Abuse, misapplication, or perversion of a rune's power can therefore still result in unintended outcomes and cause greater harm than good. The fundamental meanings of runes still hold, and the wise rune-worker always keeps this in mind.

SIMILARITY TO OGHAM

Ogham, the tree alphabet of the Celts, can be mistaken for runes and vice-versa. Both were carved on twigs and stones and were used for the same purposes, which is hardly surprising given that the Norse and Celts were close cousins and overlapped izn spheres of influence. The druids were direct counterparts to vitkar, following the shamanic way, and cast the ogham staves for divination in much the same way as rune-masters.

Ogham differs from runes in these ways: the 20 ogham letters are read vertically and are carved along one stave or line, each stave believed to represent one sentence. The letters are scored by notching parallel or slightly angled lines at intervals. Longer intervals between notches indicate a new word beginning.

What is Galdr?

Also known as "galdor," galdr is the use of magical invocations or the creation of rune-staves and signs (runes etched or burned in wood). Galdr is often used in the creation of runes, bind runes, and magical runic signs. In other words, galdr is the vocal element of Norse spells and spellwork. It can be used in seiðr, spá, and in rune-work.

Rune Poems and Rune Galdr

Rune poems are gnomic verses that, upon meditation, reveal the nature and energies of the rune's energies through kennings (the alternative name or description of a thing, person, or concept). There's also Odin's rune poems in the Hávamál.

Rune poems are not often used in incantations but may be used in meditation.

The galdr part of rune-work is a chant or song. Often these songs are composed of the sounds in the name of the rune. This may be the letter sound, or a breaking down of the rune's name into rhythm and repetition. So, for Laguz the galdr might be chanted as: La, la, la, laguz. La, la, la, gu, gu, guzzz, etc.

More About the Staves

Rune staves or magic staves were the written part of a rune spell that was etched onto wood, bone, stone, or metal. They can also be written on parchment or paper. A magical stave is formed when the written part of the spell and the galdr song work together to create a powerful spell. Staves can then be used as talismans.

PART II
THE RUNES

CHAPTER 6
THE FUTHARK— RUNIC ALPHABET

The Norse Elder Futhark or runic alphabet is generally composed of 24 runes much like the English alphabet has 26. However, there are other runic systems with the number of runes ranging from 16 to 33. Some pseudo runic writing and marks were created in the early 19th century by occult enthusiasts. (Howard, 1980).

ELDER AND YOUNGER FUTHARK

The Elder Futhark, besides being older, is the rune system traditionally used by the Norse with its 24 runes. The Younger Futhark was traditionally Germanic, being more popular in England, Germany, and adjoining countries. The Younger Futhark, with its 16 runes, is regarded as being easier to read, or an abridged version, depending on the personal preference of the rune user.

The Younger Futhark adds the meanings of the discarded runes to similar runes, for instance, the Younger Futhark ascribes the meaning and energies of Jera ᛉ (year, harvest) to Ar ᛅ (a good year).

In addition to these two systems, regional variations exist often with influences from local alphabets and more ancient symbols. Some divination systems also ascribe specific runic letters a divinatory meaning where the Elder Futhark was unknown or not employed.

FYI: THE FUTHARK

The Futhark, or Futhorc, derives its name from the sound of the first six Norse runes: Fehu (F), Uruz (U), Thorn (TH), Ansuz (A), Raidho (R), and Kenaz (K), and is believed to have been in use from about 200 B.C.E. (Thorssen, 1993).

The 24 runes are divided into three sets of eight runes. The first set, or aett, belongs to Freya, concerning life's cycle from conception to death. The second aett belongs to Hagalaz, or Heimdall, concerning the outer world and its impact on life. The third set belongs to Tiwaz, concerning the response to the outer world by inner strength and wisdom.

CORRESPONDENCE IN WRITING

Runes began as magical or primal symbols, only being used for writing accounts and mundane messages after the 10th century C.E.. Each rune lends its sound to phonetics, with a couple of runes hosting two letters. These phonetics could differ among regions. Add the regional differences in runic styles, and you have various interpretations of the same rune sentences. Generally, though, the standard Norse runes to letters reads like this:

Rune	Name	Letter
ᚠ	Fehu	f
ᚢ	Uruz	u
ᚦ	Thorn	th
ᚨ	Ansuz	a
ᚱ	Raidho	r
ᚲ	Kenaz	k
ᚷ	Gebo	g
ᚹ	Wunjo	w
ᚺ	Hagalaz	h

Rune	Name	Sound
ᚾ	Naudhiz	n
ᛁ	Isa	i
ᛃ	Jera	j or y
ᛇ	Eiwaz	i
ᛈ	Perthro	p
ᛉ	Elhaz	z
ᛋ	Sowilo	s
ᛏ	Tiwaz	t
ᛒ	Berkano	b
ᛖ	Ehwaz	E
ᛗ	Mannaz	m
ᛚ	Laguz	l
ᛜ	Ingwaz	ng
ᛞ	Dagaz	d
ᛟ	Othala	o

NOTE ON THE ELDER AND YOUNGER FUTHARK DIFFERENCES

The differences in Elder and Younger Futharks are the following:

Deleted from the Younger Futhark: Gebo, Wunjo, Jera, Perthro, Ehwaz, Ing, Dagaz, Othala.

Differences to the Elder Futhark: As (Ansuz), Kaun (Kenaz), Hagall (Hagalaz), Ar (jera), Sol (Sowilo), Madhr (Mannaz), Yr (Eihwaz). Note that the meanings for Kaun/Kenaz, Ar/Jera, Madhr/Mannaz are changed in the Younger Futhark.

INDIVIDUAL RUNE MEANINGS

We'll be using the Elder Futhark runes and meanings with its 24 runes. With this knowledge you can easily adapt to the 16 rune system of the Younger Futhark.

FEHU ᚠ

ALSO SPELLED: Feoh or Fé

LETTER: F

CALENDAR RUNE: September: the shedding month of the Wood Moon

SET OF: Freya

LITERAL MEANING: Drizzle

KEYWORDS
Cattle/stock, wealth, financial abundance, cost, worth, riches, value, money, fee

GENERAL MEANING
Two concepts lie in the rune, Fehu—comfort, and the price of comfort. For the Norse, cattle was representative of wealth or the means to greater wealth. The more cattle you had, the more prosperous you were. With wealth came comfort. And with comfort (some of the old rune poems warn) came strife, worry, and a danger to comfort. After all, the more cattle you had, the more likely your herd would be rustled away by thieves, or that your neighbors would challenge you for grazing land.

So, Fehu asks: What the true cost of your prosperity?

Contemplation of Fehu can enlighten you to the bigger picture, and so to the hidden cost of your decisions and actions.

Fehu also signifies flowing wealth and vitality. Both have to be exchanged and allowed to flow in and out—to give and receive—in order for it to circulate and grow. Hoarding energy or wealth will prevent this freeflow and cause blockages in the situation, turning a good situation toxic.

Some ascribe an energy of creation or amplification to Fehu, intensifying the power of runes surrounding it.

Fehu/Feoh can also refer to a person who is practical as well as heart-based, grounded, and with practical, achievable solutions. If these are the qualities you wish to seed in your magic work, Fehu will help you.

Divinatory Meaning

The positive: Matters concerning wealth are well aligned, but they can generate conflicts. New beginnings and foundations are possible.

The negative: Greed is at play—yours or anothers. A lack of generosity or stinginess will result in toxicity and sabotage the subject.

Uruz ᚢ

ALSO SPELLED: Ur

LETTER: U

CALENDAR RUNE: February of the Horn Moon

SET OF: Freya

LITERAL MEANING: Drizzle

KEYWORDS
Strength, primal, primordial forces, courage, endurance, overcoming hardships, single-mindedness, stubbornness, instincts

GENERAL MEANING
Besides the immense strength of body, mind, and spirit, Uruz also talks about cultivation and progress by working through annoyances and adverse conditions. In fact, adverse conditions may create conditions that force creativity and refinement. In the rune poem of Uruz, drizzle is the adversity faced by herders, forcing them to think on their feet to keep their herd together and get them home safely.

Uruz is linked to the primordial energies of creation as it's linked to Audhumla, the primal cow, who sustained the first ice giant, Ymir, and who—by licking the primordial ice—created Buri, the grandfather of Odin.

So, Uruz asks do you have the strength to overcome all of the hurdles to what you seek, no matter how tough the going gets?

Uruz can refer to a person who is single-minded, displays exceptional will power, overcomes through perseverance, and is success-driven.

Divinatory meaning

The positive: Progress is strong. Career ambitions are attainable, and generally matters will go well. Good health and happiness are yours. Endurance and routine work will reward you greatly.

The negative: Ill health and toxicity or manipulation is dragging you down. Seek help or treatment, address toxic patterns early, and be aware of manipulation. Ill fortune and adverse influences or conditions may slow your progress or introduce obstacles. Beware of what and how you create at this time.

Thurisaz ᚦ

Also spelled: Thurs, Thorn

Letter: Th or X

Calendar rune: No

Set of: Freya

Literal meaning: Thorn, giant, Thor's hammer

Keywords
Protection, opposition, natural enemy, resistance, defensive, secrecy

General meaning
Thurisaz has three possible meanings. As thorn, it provides protection, but at a cost. Yes, the thorn tree provides protection, but you may get scratched and bleed in order to receive that protection.

As the giant, Thurs, it questions and opposes the new, being quintessentially old school and against changes to any order. If you're to gain from the actions or inactions, another, who is to lose, is sure to oppose it. And while change may be necessary, there will always be those who will seek to delay or challenge it.

As a representation of the god Thor's hammer, Thurisaz blesses blóts and offers the god's protection.

Thurisaz asks: What needs the most protection? Is it worth protecting? Who or what is in opposition?

Divinatory meaning
The positive: Good news comes, especially from abroad or a vast distance. A trip across water will go well. You and yours are protected.

The negative: Delays in journeys. A tough journey is likely. You may want to schedule your travel for another time. Unpleasant news is arriving. Prepare yourself.

Ansuz ᚨ

Also spelled: Asa, Os, Ásse

Letter: A

Calendar rune: No

Set of: Freya

Literal meaning: A god

Keywords
Communication, patterns, consciousness, wisdom. poetic prowess, sovereignty, ancestry

General meaning
Also known as Odin the All Father's rune, Ansuz holds the energies of Odin's quest for all-encompassing wisdom and all-powerful words. He sacrificed his eye for wisdom, and his integrity when he deceived and stole the mead that bestows the gift of poetry and powerful words.

Ansuz also speaks of patterns and consciousness. Be consciously aware of patterns, or allow unconscious and hidden patterns to be discerned through integrated knowledge.

Ansuz asks: Will your words be hollow? What is the pattern?

Divinatory meaning

The positive: Inspiration, knowledge and the holistic approach works best by relying on your intuition plus the information and wisdom you hold. Knowledge passed on from an elder will aid you.

The negative: Delusions and misunderstanding may cost you more than you realize. Beware of deliberate miscommunication. Bad advice surrounds you, particularly from one posing as all-knowing.

Raidho R

Also spelled: Rad, Reidh

Letter: R

Calendar rune: April of the Cuckoo Moon

Set of: Freya

Literal meaning: Riding, wheel

Keywords
Travel, ascension, wheels, cycles, journeys, life, phases of life, rewards, commerce, motor, transport

General meaning
A long journey over land. Raidho carries the energies of riding across difficult terrain on horseback. It would have been considered swift movement compared to travel by foot. These days, it may literally reference motor vehicles, especially powerful ones.

Another interpretation of Raidho is that of a wheel—the wheel of a vehicle as well as the cycles in nature. The turning of the wheel of life brings you closer to ascension to Valhalla or a descent to Hel.

Raidho asks: If life is a difficult journey for you, what of those who bear your burdens, too?

The rune could refer to an adventurer or pioneer—someone who is motivated by exploration and realizing their dreams.

Divinatory meaning

The positive: A significant journey will lead to happiness and reward. Your current happiness is a journey, not a destination. Unexpected assistance or support arrives. You don't have to journey alone. An institution is significant to the issues. Speedy results and rewards.

The negative: Sudden journeys because of illness or family drama, a crisis, irrationality, blockages to movement.

KENAZ <

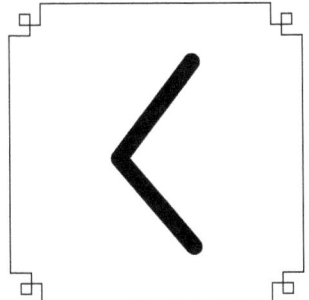

ALSO SPELLED: Ken, Kaun, Kano

LETTER: K

CALENDAR RUNE: No

SET OF: Freya

LITERAL MEANING: Torch, fire

KEYWORDS
Fire, destruction, analyzing, light, explosion, creation, procreation, fertility

GENERAL MEANING
Kenaz is energy in its most potent form. It can cause destruction or it can create in equal time and to the same degree. Whether it's physical, creative, or magical energy, Kenaz can make you or destroy you. To control this energy or to master it brings unlimited potential to create anew. It's the volcano and the wildfire, but also the hearth fire and the heat of passion. In its destructive form, Kenaz dissolves bonds and reduces materials to their essences. It's a crucible, though maybe a cruel one if used carelessly. Kenaz asks: What will you create that won't fizzle out? How will you stop your passions from consuming you?

DIVINATORY MEANING

The positive: Creative inspiration is yours. Use it wisely and manage it or it will fizzle out or consume you. Time out for relaxation and refueling is here. Clarity and a burning sense of purpose have arrived.

The negative: You may be burned out from overwork, burning the candle at both ends or overindulging in sex. Confusion from a multitude of ideas or a lack of vision slows your progress or destroys an opportunity. You may be consumed by ambition, creative vision, lust or love, or anger. Anger or rage is ruling your decisions.

Gebo X

Also spelled: Gyfu

Letter: G

Calendar rune: No

Set of: Freya

Literal meaning: Gift

Keywords
Gift, reciprocity, union, giving, contracts, swap, love and sexual relationships, mutual beneficial agreements, favors, divine blessings, sacrificial gift

General meaning
Giving and receiving with expectation is the energy of Gebo. The expectation is that generosity and graciousness would be remembered and returned in equal amounts. Naturally, a valuable gift would mean a favor may be requested in the future, one that would not be denied.

Gebo also refers to loving and sexual unions in and out of wedlock, marriage contracts, and promises exchanged. Divine blessings and favor are another message of Gebo. The exchange of information and insight can also be a meaning of Gebo.

Gebo asks: Is there mutual generosity in the situation? If not, can there ever be balance and harmony?

A seldom-used meaning of Gebo is a sacrifice to a god or seeking divine favor through a sacrifice.

Divinatory meaning

The positive: Marriage and weddings, a gift signifying kindredness, love and happiness

The negative: Unhappiness in love or relationships, overgiving, stinginess, a gift given with questionable motives

Wunjo ᚹ

ALSO SPELLED: Wyn, Wynn

LETTER: V or W

CALENDAR RUNE: No

SET OF: Freya

LITERAL MEANING: Joy

Keywords
Joy, happiness, glory

General meaning
Wunjo speaks of joy that's found when you experience happiness and acceptance through self-realization. Knowing yourself and your place in your environment, your community, and the universe offers pathways and experiences of joy you may not otherwise see.

Inner harmony comes from a healthy sense of self-worth. Wunjo highlights that your worth may be higher than you think. Inner harmony leads to more joy and happiness.

Success and strength stemming from your sense of inner harmony and being at peace with your place in the world is also a message of Wunjo.

Another meaning of wunjo is finding joy in the simpler and natural things in life.

Wunjo asks: If you cannot find joy and happiness, where have you not looked?

Divinatory meaning
The positive: Joy and happiness, a distressing period transforms into a happier time.

The negative: Unearned entitlement, loss of love, self-aggrandizement.

HAGALAZ ᚺ

ALSO SPELLED: Haegl, Hagall

LETTER: H

CALENDAR RUNE: December of the Wolf Moon

SET OF: Hagalaz or Heimdall

LITERAL MEANING: Hail, disruption

KEYWORDS
Hail, change, snow, seed, frozen potential, darkest hour ending, destruction, a sudden crisis, potential for change

GENERAL MEANING
By carrying the energies of the destructive power of hail and destruction of what you may have planted—figuratively and materially—this rune may not always be welcomed. However, there are other energies that are also fundamental to Hagalaz.

Often referred to as the "cold grain" (from the Rune Poems) and "cosmic seed," Hagalaz signifies great potential and outcomes, providing changes are made and cosmic rules observed. (Thorrson, 1993. Easson, 1997).

Like Thurs, Hagalaz can also be called upon for protection or as a weapon, but remember that the nature of the runes will always exact a price for such uses.

Hagalaz could suggest a person who is a dreamer and a visionary, but who is still to act or reluctant to make their dreams materialize.

The question Hagalaz asks is: What changes need to occur to unlock this potential?

DIVINATORY MEANING
The positive: Delays favor you or work to your benefit.

The negative: Unforeseen and uncontrollable delays and setbacks.

Naudhiz ᚾ

Also spelled: Nyd, Naudh

Letter: N

Calendar rune: No

Set of: Hagalaz or Heimdall

Literal meaning: Need

Keywords
Need, lack, needful, fateful, compulsion, destiny, caution, friction, passion, opposition

General meaning
Naudhiz embodies the compulsion to fill a void. Most times, the void it references is the one within yourself. The gift of Naudhiz is the revealing of your strength, intelligence, and discernment during tough times.

While it may also reveal those forces and persons that oppose you or the action, it also reveals the hand of fate or destiny at work. Some things need to happen despite your need to control. Naudhiz teaches you the hard lesson of holding onto only what is needful, working with only the necessary, and flowing with events you can't control.

"Needfire" is another meaning of Naudhiz. (Thorsson, 1993). Needfire, kindled at the start of the year or at ceremonies, was produced by friction; the spark growing into fire and warmth that made survival and comfort possible. Therefore, by capturing the energy created by the friction or resistance in a situation, you can still produce a satisfying outcome.

Naudhiz asks: Where does the friction stem from and how can the energy it creates be harnessed?

Naudhiz may refer to a person who's an eternal seeker or insatiable in some way. They are always seeking to fill a perceived void in their life.

Divinatory meaning

The positive: Proceed cautiously. Do only what is needful. Take note if you're fulfilling all needs. Regeneration through invention.

The negative: Rushing into decisions and actions leads to disaster. Excessiveness leads to regret and hardships.

ISA |

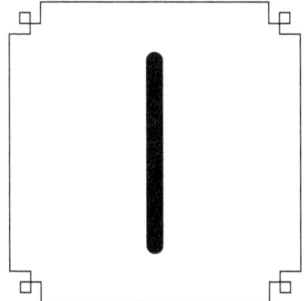

ALSO SPELLED: Is, Iss, Isaz

LETTER: V or W

CALENDAR RUNE: January of the Snow Moon

SET OF: Hagalaz or Heimdall

LITERAL MEANING: Ice

KEYWORDS
Ice, stillness, bridging, harshness, trap, contraction, stagnancy, focusing, a freeze, hibernation, isolation

GENERAL MEANING
Isa exemplifies the energies of the cold before the thaw. Change is anticipated, but no action can be taken until the right time or another's timetable has been reached. Isa therefore counsels using the time wisely when waiting on someone or something. It's a time for strategizing, planning, and reflecting.

Referring to the ice across waters, Isa can also be read as a bridge, a causeway that can be accessed with caution to explore other dimensions and possibilities.

Strangely, Isa may also provide an element of safety in certain circumstances where conditions prevent others accessing you or your resources.

It's also believed that with its solitary line, Isa's energies are found in most other runes to a greater or lesser degree.

Isa asks: Have you done enough to prepare for what comes next?

Isa could refer to a person who wields wisdom and bides their time until the optimal time to act is reached. They also have deep, hidden reserves of resources they may call upon.

Divinatory meaning

The positive: Containment of a situation, delay, or a halt is beneficial at this time.

The negative: Treacherous conditions, entrapment, impasse, isolation.

JERA

ALSO SPELLED: Ár, Ger

LETTER: J

CALENDAR RUNE: No

SET OF: Hagalaz or Heimdall

LITERAL MEANING: Year, harvest

KEYWORDS: A cycle, life cycles, bounty, reaping what you sow, natural phases, cyclic events, fertility

GENERAL MEANING

Jera holds the energy of profit based on the work put in and tempered by the cycles of life and the wisdom you've applied to the situation. The profits may be good, or they could be meager.

Generally, Jera's message is welcomed as it often speaks of good—peace accompanying prosperity, welcome rewards after hard work, and fertility of field and family.

It also refers to maturity and a comfortable retirement, building on your wisdom from the past. However, representing the hand of fate, Jera can also indicate your rewards may be affected by external factors—bad weather on a good and well-tended crop.

Jera asks: When you're unsatisfied with your reward, why do you repeat the same mistakes and actions?

Jera may hint of a person who's aware of natural cycles, and, by honoring these cycles, finds peace and prosperity no matter what their neighbors experience.

DIVINATORY MEANING

The positive: A good harvest, peace, rewards for efforts, plenty, a good year, a caution to hold your judgment on others until facts are verified.

The negative: Lack, poverty, little return for great efforts, conflict, a bad year, and an argument that may end a relationship.

Eihwaz ᛇ

Also spelled: Eiwaz, Yr, Iwaz

Letter: Y

Calendar rune: No

Set of: Hagalaz or Heimdall

Literal meaning: Yew

Keywords: Potential contained or restrained, duality, death, life, extreme polar opposites, visions, shamanistic magic. weapon (the bow)

General meaning

The yew tree demands respect, and any prudent Norse was sure to treat it with deference. Not only does the long-living tree provide life-giving warmth and food with its wood for burning and making bows, but it also provides a deadly substance that steals life from you or your enemies. Eihwaz can, like so many runes, be a double-edged sword with some using it to cast poisonous spells. Whenever using Eihwaz, be aware that it signals the bridging of Middle Earth (Midgard) with the gods and beings of the upper and lower realms. Communication with these beings can be facilitated using this rune.

Eihwaz asks: If you choose the light or the dark, what about the in-between?

Personality wise, Eihwaz may refer to a person of uncertain benevolence—one who may save as well as destroy. It could also refer to one who practices magic or holds power that can be wielded to uncertain effect.

Divinatory meaning

The positive: Resolution of a persistent problem, messages about or from an old acquaintance.

The negative: A resumption of hostilities in a situation or relationship.

PERTHRO ᛈ

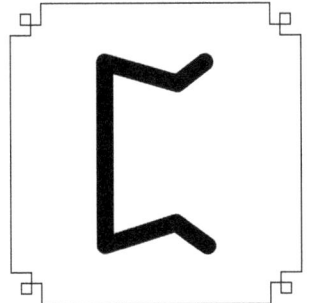

ALSO SPELLED: Perth, Peorth, Pear

LETTER: P

CALENDAR RUNE: May of the Merry Moon

SET OF: Hagalaz or Heimdall

LITERAL MEANING: Lot-cup

KEYWORDS: Core self, unperceived, enigma, predestination or personal destiny, testing boundaries, pushing luck, a gamble

GENERAL MEANING

In some sets that don't use the blank wyrd stone, Perthro assumes the same unknown mysterious energy.

Representing the Norns, or the Three Fates, Perthro carries the energies of fate and the will of the gods and universe. Once you've drawn your lot or cards of life, it's up to you to make the best of it all.

Perthro's energy is used to discover and refine your core self—the essence of your being. By throwing you curveballs and sticking you on the path of what's destined to meet you, Perthro keeps you on your toes and continually evolving.

The energy of Perthro points to a possible gamble or a risky way of making a big change. What the outcome will be if you choose to take action will remain unknown until the hand of fate reveals itself.

Perthro asks: How will you play your cards? Where or with whom will you cast in your lot?

Perthro can also speak of a person who's highly principled and distinguished in some way.

This mystery rune can also indicate that there are larger forces or players in the game that you cannot influence at this time.

Divinatory meaning

The positive: A windfall from an unexpected event or source.

The negative: Damage to your reputation through an invasion of privacy or a secret that surfaces.

ELHAZ ᛉ

ALSO SPELLED: Algiz

LETTER: z

CALENDAR RUNE: No

SET OF: Hagalaz or Heimdall

LITERAL MEANING: Elk, double-edged sword

KEYWORDS: Duality, protection, needing careful handling, defense

GENERAL MEANING

The energy of Elhaz is another that must be handled with care and respect. Said to resemble the elk horns, a splayed out hand, and a double-edged sword, this rune can provide great protection, but also has the capacity to simultaneously deplete or hurt you.

Elhaz also wields the power of duality, particularly within yourself. You can protect and defend, or attack and destroy. You can heal and you can hurt, sometimes simultaneously.

In the rune poems, Elhaz is likened to eelgrass: Difficult and painful to harvest, but providing greater long-term benefits. (Eason, 1998).

Elhaz asks: When wielding a double-edged sword, which side should you favor?

Elhaz also cautions that important matters are at a fragile state and need careful handling.

DIVINATORY MEANING

The positive: Good news about your career or business, careful handling of business brings better outcomes.

The negative: Irrecoverable losses or irredeemable goods and favors.

Sowilo ᛋ

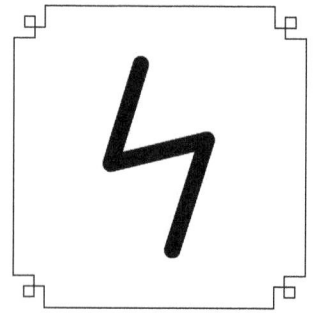

Also spelled: Sigil, Sigel

Letter: S or YZ

Calendar rune: June of the Sun Moon

Set of: Hagalaz or Heimdall

Literal meaning: The sun, the sun wheel

Keywords

The sun, impermanence, reaching for the greatest goals, energy, warmth, potential, life force, success, release, a beacon

General meaning

Sowilo embodies the energy of Sunna, the feminine force of nurturing and freedom that melts away restrictions and inertia. Sowilo energizes a situation, breeding success. The spinning radiant energy of the sun's passage across the sky is also carried in this rune, representing the sun wheel that makes all life possible.

However, the sun doesn't shine permanently in the sky, nor at the same intensity, so this rune also speaks of impermanence.

Sowilo encourages reaching for the highest possible attainable goals, pushing to reach your greatest potential, and so almost always guarantees some form of success.

This rune carries messages about the life force in you, the people around you, your enemies, and of the greater universe.

Sowilo asks: Where would applying your energy now release the most potential?

This rune could also speak of a person with great energy and creativity, a luminous personality that lives in the moment, for the moment, and prefers taking immediate action.

Divinatory meaning

The positive: Your higher self or communication from higher beings, happy achievements. Success is guaranteed in almost any endeavor.

The negative: Self-delusions cloud judgment and create roadblocks to success. Failure opens the door to new and possibly better options.

Tiwaz ↑

ALSO SPELLED: Tyr, Tiw

LETTER: T

CALENDAR RUNE: No

SET OF: Tiwaz

LITERAL MEANING: Star, sky god, god

KEYWORDS
Sacrifice, altruism, wounded warrior, war, stamina, courage, noble, leader, cosmic order and hierarchy, justice, loyalty, conceding to another

GENERAL MEANING
Tiwaz draws in the energies of loyalty, courage, and faithfulness to empower and stabilize a community or relationship.

Embodying aspects of the energy that helped create the universe and then structure it with law and order, Tiwaz is a fiercely strong rune that connects to male energies as well as the logical flow of creations and their place in the universe.

Fairness or justice is sought by this rune, often judiciously and with great consideration to the parties involved and the wellbeing of the community.

Sacrifice and self-sacrifice is another large aspect of Tiwaz, illustrated by the god Tiw placing his hand in the wolf Fenris' mouth as surety that Odin and its family wasn't entrapping it. Tiw accepted the loss of his arm that prevented him from challenging Odin in the future as the leader of the tribe.

Tiwaz asks: How can you institute law and order without destroying what's already working?

Divinatory meaning

The positive: An amorous relationship will grow into a lasting bond. Everything is as it should be. A seeming handicap is in fact a strength. Justice rules.

The negative: Playing with affections and spreading love around thinly leads only to heartbreak. Manipulation by another. Justice is not assured.

BERKANO ᛒ

ALSO SPELLED: Beorc, Bjarkan

LETTER: B

CALENDAR RUNE: March of the Mother Moon

SET OF: Tiwaz

LITERAL MEANING: Birch, Earth/Birch Mother

KEYWORDS
Birth, fertility, beginning, renewal, motherhood, recolonizing, transformation.

GENERAL MEANING
Berkano, also often referred to as "beorc," embodies the energies of the birch tree and Birch Tree Mother. The Norse claim that the birch tree was the first to recolonize the land after the ice of the last ice age receded. With the birch tree being the first tree to regenerate its canopy in spring, berkano brings this energy of regeneration and optimism. The Birch Tree Mother refers to the ancient Earth Mother goddess who protected and brought fertility to the land. Birch trees were therefore sacred to the Norse and the Celts who used birch switches to hit those wishing to conceive babies in an ancient fertility ritual.

Transformation, personal and in the environment, is another energy of Berkano. This transformation may bring new opportunities and new life to an old relationship or situation.

Berkano can also hold protection afforded by the Earth Mother in her many forms.

Berkano asks: What needs new birthing? Will transformation bring the renewal or the new beginning you seek?

This rune may also refer to a person who is very creative and remains optimistic no matter the situation. They are also very loving and affectionate.

DIVINATORY MEANING

The positive: The beginning or birth of a new idea or new life. A marriage. Fertility. Natural regrowth and processes.

The negative: Infertility, divorce, or loss of a beginning or a new life. Canceling of contracts or new agreements. Lack of growth and stagnation.

EHWAZ (HORSE) ᛖ

ALSO SPELLED: Eh

LETTER: E

CALENDAR RUNE: October of the Hunting Moon

SET OF: Tiwaz

LITERAL MEANING: Horse

KEYWORDS
Teamwork, harmony, work-mate, inner peace, camaraderie, travel, companionship.

GENERAL MEANING
Signifying the horse for which the Norse had a sense of camaraderie and affection, Ehwaz carries the energy of harmony and a healthy codependency.

Ehwaz speaks of teamwork, and how, together, journeys become less tedious and are more likely to be successful.

Faithful companionship is another message of Ehwaz. The Norse treated their horses with great regard and honor, even giving them elaborate burials. A horse was not just a means of transport, but a companion through adventures, and an ally in battles.

With Raidho also appearing, it may also refer to companionship during a journey.

Ehwaz asks: Who can you trust to remain by your side no matter the circumstances?

Ehwaz may also refer to a person who is balanced in their thinking and views, often seeing both sides of an argument or dispute. They may also appear unaffected by disharmony around them as they carry their own system of personal peace.

Divinatory meaning

The positive: A trustworthy, hardworking companion. A swift journey resulting from cooperation. A large distance covered. Ehwaz can also speak of a successful relocation or change in career.

The negative: Untrustworthy individuals or companions around you. A delay in journeys, or a slow, tiring journey. A shorter distance covered than expected. Obstacles in the path of relocating or changing career.

Mannaz ᛗ

Also spelled: Madhr

Letter: M

Calendar rune: No

Set of: Tiwaz

Literal meaning: Man, mankind

Keywords
A tribesperson, ancestry, web of relationships, inheritance, collective consciousness, genetic memory

General meaning
Mannaz carries the joint energies of mortality and immortality—the mortality of a person, their deeds, and their impact on the world around them carrying into immortality. It also simultaneously embodies the web of connection to our families, our tribes, our ancestral past, and to all of humanity.

This rune's energy is one of compassion and understanding of human frailty, imperfection, ingenuity, intelligence, and endurance.

Mannaz asks: Where do you fit in humankind's family? Which traditions serve your growth and the future best at this time? For what you create now will persist in some form or the other.

Divinatory meaning
The positive: The enquirer, a growing perspective of the world around you. Interaction with people outside your tribe, culture, or geographical area.

The negative: Hermit-mode, retreating to meditate, learn, or to germinate new ideas.

Laguz ᛚ

Also spelled: Lögr, Lagu

Letter: L

Calendar rune: No

Set of: Tiwaz

Literal meaning: Water, life force

Keywords
Life force, feelings, nourishment, intuition, inspiration, precognitive dreams, initiation

General meaning
Laguz carries the energies of the primeval soup from which all of life originates—the amniotic fluid that fills and nourishes nascent life.

The appearance of Laguz informs that intuition and going with the flow is key.

Signifying water, Laguz can also literally refer to bodies of water, rivers, and streams.

Another strong energy of this rune is the well of feelings and emotions that can either lift you up or drown you.

Laguz is therefore an important rune for initiation into the spiritual and magical worlds, building strength in individuals that's very different from the strength of uruz and tiw.

Laguz asks: Where will these emotions lead? What are you resisting that should be allowed to flow?

Divinatory meaning
The positive: Predictive dreams, a significant woman.
The negative: A woman complicates matters.

INGWAZ ◇

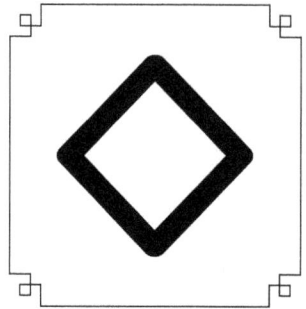

ALSO SPELLED: Ing, Yng

LETTER: None

CALENDAR RUNE: August of the Harvest Moon

SET OF: Tiw

LITERAL MEANING: Ing—a deity, god of corn

KEYWORDS: Fertility, protection, gestation, agriculture, holistic approach, twin realms of the magical and the mundane, the hearth, home or homeland, cycles of fertility and productivity, rebirth, renewal, sustainability, resting, hibernation

GENERAL MEANING

Similar to the other fertility runes, especially Jera, Ingwaz carries the energies of cycles and processes that require time and specific steps in order to yield a goal.

The ancient corn god, Ing, was the consort of the Earth Mother, Nerthus, and echoes the rune Berkano's energies of birth and renewal.

Hibernation or a period of rest between producing and renewal is also a message of Ing. The god Ing annually died in August after the harvest and rebirthed during the winter solstice in order to flourish the crops through spring and summer. Ing can therefore refer to hibernation and necessary rest in order to continue successfully.

Ing brings protection of the home and homestead, as well as the warmth and practicality of the home fireplace.

Ing asks: What needs to go into hibernation to grow or produce even more?

This rune may also refer to a place seen as home or a place to settle into. It can also hint at the magic in the mundane, or the intermingling of magical and everyday concerns and solutions.

Divinatory meaning

The positive: News about someone from a distance to you, news from your homeland. Your home is protected.

The negative: Your communication is lost, mistranslated, or meets no response. Danger to your home or community from fires.

Dagaz ᛞ

Also spelled: Daeg, Dueg

Letter: D

Calendar rune: July of the Hay Moon

Set of: Tiw

Literal meaning: Day, awakening

Keywords
Illumination, enlightenment, faith, clarity, summer solstice, paradox, perfect balance

General meaning
Dagaz carries the energies of the transitioning of light periods—sunrise, sunset, and midday.

It may also speak of harmony between seemingly irreconcilable differences and a turning point in a challenging situation, marking a period when things get significantly better.

With Dagaz, two opposing forces are perfectly balanced or in harmony. The situation may be delicate and may not last long.

Dagaz asks: Now that you can see the situation so clearly, how does your point of view change?

This rune may refer to a person who's optimistic and believes in the inherent good of the people and world around them.

Divinatory meaning
The positive: Faith brings respite and a lighter situation. A spotlight on the event or person. Transitions into natural cycles.

The negative: People attempt to cause fear and misunderstandings, warmth and renewal is slow to arrive, climate change affects matters adversely.

OTHALA ᛟ

ALSO SPELLED: Odal, Othalan

LETTER: O

CALENDAR RUNE: November of the Fog Moon

SET OF: Tiw

LITERAL MEANING: Home, homestead

KEYWORDS
Retirement, family inheritances, family estates, family burdens, ancestral help

GENERAL MEANING
Othala carries the energies of close community and family ties, building a progression and future together. It also embodies energies of home comforts as a reward to long, hard work—everyday comforts, rather than fantastic riches.

This rune speaks of strong foundations and stability, especially on the mundane level that affects home life and relationships.

Othala asks: How can you build on what has come before?

Othala can refer to a person who loves their home, homeland, and has a strong, spiritual and emotional connection to the land. They are also an excellent host and may be creative in producing comfortable homesettings.

It can also refer to an elder or a family member in need of care.

DIVINATORY MEANING

The positive: A good retirement, reading of a will, an inheritance.

The negative: A selfish older person, or one who's being overly burdensome.

The Wyrd

Also spelled: Weird

Letter: Non

Calendar rune: None

Set of: None

Literal meaning: The Unknown, the unknowable.

Some rune sets use a blank rune to signify the greater web of energies and the universe that we remain unaware of, but that might still affect our affairs. Wyrd can be thought of as untamed magic, the unknown and the unknowable, or the fate that cannot yet be revealed.

If a rune set doesn't utilize the blank Wyrd stone, the mysterious unknown and unknowable is represented by Perthro.

CHAPTER 7
CASTING RUNES FOR DIVINATION

F or millennia, runes have been consulted over matters of state, marriage, commerce, crops, and the outcomes of endeavors by people and gods. They forecast, advise, and forewarn, but only to a point. Not all of destiny can be revealed; only the querent's fate. Prophecy of the larger destinies of gods, heroes, and the worlds were the province of völvur discerning the webs of wyrd in their seiðr visions.

Rune-masters also studied and practiced seiðr, accessing a rune's energy directly for divination and magical purposes. For rune-casting, meditation and purification are advised, but not as deeply as for a seiðr seeing.

About Casting Runes for Divination

As mentioned before, casting or reading the runes for trivial matters isn't advised. "A gift for a gift" still applies, the gift given being knowledge—Odin's greatest treasure—and so the gift you send back must be of equal energy. Gods and primal energies are not to be short-changed, ever.

How Rune Reading Differs From Tarot

With runes often inscribed on card and paper these days, it's easy to regard them as regular oracle and tarot cards. While this may be fine to a certain extent, the rules of rune-reading and divination still apply. They may look like similar systems, and may even be presented and used as such, but their differences are greater than their similarities.

Tarot uses depictions of universal archetypes and symbols of people and human situations, adds the divine and angelic, and speaks most clearly to your everyday and spiritual life.

Runes embody universal, primal energies—the elements that make up the cosmos, the inner and outer worlds, the keystones of creation. They do also embody human concerns, but only those we share with the gods and the animal and plant kingdoms. Runes are therefore detached from the human experience, while tarot is intricately entwined in the human experience.

Asking the tarot and the runes the same question will give you very different, but equally valuable answers. The tarot's focus will be you, your circle, and events pertaining to your life. The runes will focus on your energies, the energies—human and other—that surround you, and the seasonal or collective events that will mark that period in your life. In other words, the runes say: This is the thing; it will look like this and have this effect. The tarot says: This thing may happen in this way and you'll feel and respond to it in this way.

Runes and tarot share their information from the wyrd, and both will only reveal a destiny up to a point.

Reading the tarot is therefore a great tool to explore yourself and possibilities. Studying the runes brings you that same self-growth, while reading them brings you information to help you make the best and most unemotional decisions at the time.

While the tarot has more cards and symbols to integrate before reading and divining, it is generally thought of as the more approachable and easier system to use. It requires less intense and long-term study and generally doesn't involve "a gift for a gift" exchanges, especially if you read for yourself. It's more forgiving of trivial divination and can, at times, show a sense of humor.

While runes are renowned for their magic and primal energies to actively influence outcomes and people, tarot—though sometimes used in magic—is most often a means of divination with less potent magical energies.

PREPARATION FOR RUNE DIVINATION

Naturally, you'll need runes in order to divine with them. It's imperative that you use your own set and not that of other runemasters because the runes need to be attuned to your energy and vice-versa to get a true divination.

Preparing your rune set depends on how long you've had them and how many divinations and magic-workings you've done. You may only need to cleanse the runes if you haven't used them recently. If you've just made or bought the runes, you may need to cleanse and empower the runes before you divine with them.

MAKING YOUR OWN RUNES VS BUYING A RUNE SET

Buying a rune set is very easy and convenient compared to making one of your own. You can start divinations immediately with clearly visible and standardized rune stones or pieces.

Mass-produced sets may appear quite affordable, too, until you take into account the environmental impact, including shipping, and the fact that they don't hold much of the rune's energies.

While custom-made rune sets may be more potent and quite beautiful, it's best—and most affordable, generally—to make your own. Runes hold elemental energies and sometimes simple is best.

Runes made by your hand with your energy and focus are intrinsically attuned to you, not a manufacturer, and not another rune-master. Besides making your rune-work easier, this attunement will make your rune-work much more powerful, too.

Making Your Own Rune Set

It's very simple, and often best, to make your own rune sets using stones or wood you've gathered yourself. Metal, while used in modern rune-sets, was seldom used for making runes to cast when their magical use was at its height. (Actually, runes were only first inscribed on metal objects as a makers' stamp or as a talisman after 100 C.E.) Some like to use crystals for rune stones. If you choose crystals to make your rune set, keep in mind that not all crystals will like to hold the rune energy assigned to them. If their inherent energy is opposite of the rune's, the crystal may shatter. It would therefore be best to use clear quartz for rune sets as they'll be the most likely to easily accept the programming of the rune they're asked to host.

Wood runes are best made out of hazel, ash, and oak—the trees linked to Yggdrasil, Odin, and healing. Cut a branch into discs. Using a marker or paint, write the runes. Alternatively, carve or burn the runes in. Whilst doing so, meditate on the rune you're creating and all that you know about it. This process—carving and empowering the rune—is called *risting*.

Stones for runes are best gathered from riversides, lakesides, lochs' beaches, and the seaside. Pick flat-sided stones of a similar size. Gather extra stones (30 or so), especially if you'd like to include a wyrd rune. Use a marker or paint to draw the runes, or use a sharp tool to etch the rune. Meditate on the energies of the rune you're creating and keep your focus exclusively on that rune.

Once you have your rune set, store it in a dedicated container or bag made from natural materials. A wooden box or a cloth bag work very well. It's recommended to keep your runes in a cool, dark place.

If you've used a marker or paint, and depending on the qualities of the stone you're using, you may have to renew the rune markings if they fade too fast. The same is true for wood runes.

Making Your Own Rune Staves

Rune staves are twigs or equal lengths of wooden sticks with runes carved on them. Often these staves have four shaved sides on which runes are risted on. Rune staves are also used in dedications and mundane communications.

To make your own rune staves, find 24 to 30 twigs or fashion the same number of wooden sticks into the equal lengths. If you're using twigs, shave off the bark from one end of it. On the planed surface, etch or burn your rune.

Traditionally, a runemaster would meditate on each rune until they resonated deeply with each one. Only then would they begin preparing the rune staves, working and focusing on one rune stave a day. In doing so, they were simultaneously empowering the rune stave. This laborious-sounding process was also used to produce bind runes and other magical staves.

Store your rune staves the same way that you store your rune stones—in a dedicated box or bag made out of natural materials. Empower your rune stones in the same way, too.

PURIFYING OR CLEANSING YOUR RUNES

Purifying or cleansing rune stones depends on the material they're made of. You can use one or two of the following methods:

- Rinse your runes in flowing water such as a clear stream, river, or even a healthy lake. You can also put them in a net or hessian bag and wash them in the sea. This method is best for stone runes and those crystals that aren't reactive to salt and which don't dissolve in water. Rain water will also work well. This method is not recommended for wood runes and staves.
- Place your rune set outside in a place that's safe and that receives plenty of sunshine, moonshine, and a breeze, if possible. Leave your runes out for at least a full day, or over a 24 hour period or more. This method can be used for any rune-set or rune staves and activates as well as purifies.

- Give your runes and staves a smoke-bath, much like smudging or saining, using the smoke of juniper branches or berries. Alternatively, use an incense that resonates with you.

ACTIVATING OR RENEWING YOUR RUNES AND RUNE STAVES

If you've employed the traditional rune stave method of meditation followed by creating a rune a day with great focus and intent, then this stage can be skipped as your rune work will already be potent and resonating with you and the energies they've been consecrated to.

If you've bought your runes or made them in a quicker manner, you must activate your runes, also known as empowering them.

- In a well-sealed box or bag made of natural materials, place your runes wrapped in a cloth. Place the box in the ground and cover with soil. Leave for at least a week or longer. This method is recommended for any rune set or staves provided the ground is not damp.

- Use the four elements—earth, fire, air and water—to activate your runes. Set out your runes on a clean cloth. Sprinkle the runes with salt to infuse with earth energies and ground them. To infuse with the element of fire, pass each rune through a candle flame, ensuring you don't burn yourself. Be especially careful with wood and other flammable runes during this process. Remember that if you used paint to mark the rune, fumes may be toxic to you, so it's best to do this process outdoors with a protected flame. To activate the element of air, pass the rune through a smoke bath of incense smoke. Finally, steep the runes in water or sprinkle rain water over all of them.

HALLOWING

Before every casting it's good practice to ensure your divining space is hallowed. You can use the methods described in *Sacred Spaces* or in the manner you feel most comfortable. This can include "saining" with smoke—sprinkling with blessed or sacred water, envisioning a circle of light purifying and holding fast the borders of the space.

MEDITATION OR SEIÐR WORK

Before you begin you may want to throw off the energies and distractions of everyday life and the day's energies by doing meditation or seiðr work. If seiðr work is not possible, a simple meditation to ground yourself, clear your energies, and establish a connection or reconnection to the runes in a conscious way will help you interpret your runes with greater clarity.

Most rune-casters prefer using a rune-cloth; a white or light square of cloth with a large circle drawn on it and a wide border. This cloth can be set on any clear, flat surface that's available.

Invoke the gods, goddesses, and your personal guides to help divine and guide you as well as protect the divination from interfering and hostile forces.

INVOCATION

Rune-masters invoked the gods before each casting. Odin and the Norns are most often called upon generally. Thor may be called in to protect and to offer advice or for weather and crop information. So, too, can Njord be called up. Freya and Frigg are also often called in for matters of the heart and motherhood. Tiw is invoked when the matter involves justice or negotiations, while Baldr is called in for those wishing a healing or for greater happiness and harmony. Loki can be invoked, too, particularly for mischief makers or those seeking mirth. The rune masters totems and other spirit guides may also be called in to assist.

If a god is invoked you must always thank them at the end of the casting. To forget their presence and guidance may be taken as a sign of disrespect. You may therefore want to plan your invocation in advance and note the deities and energies you're calling upon.

Methods of Rune Divination

Once your hallowed space is set, the rune cloth is spread and the gods and guides invoked, it's time to decide (if you haven't already) which casting to do.

When deciding, remember to take into account the time you have available. The more complicated the casting and number of runes you'll interpret can be quite time-consuming. Then, too, you may find you're unable to read the runes once they're cast. A break may be needed. Come back to the spread in a few hours or the next day and you're likely to intuit the answer much more readily then.

The Three Norns or Past, Present, Future Cast

This is the simplest cast of runes. Three runes are randomly selected from a bag or box. The runes can be cast in two ways:

- The rune-master shakes or mixes the runes in their box or bag without looking at them. When they feel ready, the rune-master selects three runes, drawing them out of the bag and casting them onto the rune-cloth. The runes are then read how and where they fall.

- In the second method, the rune-master shakes or mixes the runes in their box or bag, and not looking, draws the runes individually. The rune is then cast or placed where the rune-master feels the rune wants to lie.

The runes are read as one for each Norn. Urd's stone speaks of the past, what cannot be changed but still resonates through the situation. Verdandi's rune speaks of the present; what is currently happening, what can be changed to a certain extent depending on your attitude and the effort you put in. Skald's rune speaks of the future—what is to come, and what may be changeable, at a price.

Another three runes can be cast to gain further information on each rune. A final group of three runes can be drawn (three times threes is nine—Odin's sacred number) to provide solutions and advice.

THE GRID DIVINATION

This reading is much like the Norn's layout amplified, and can be very versatile even as it maintains structure of the reading. It also uses Odin's number—nine.

First, construct a grid. This can be on an area of your rune cloth or another grid demarcated by small twigs, stones, or even drawn on paper. Your grid must have three rows of three to fit nine runes.

The runes can be cast either individually, and without looking, by selecting a rune from the bag and assigning it a block in the set of nine as you feel, or by randomly selecting the rune and casting it on the grid to let it find its place on a row. Repeat until all the positions are filled. If one rune knocks another out, you can take note of the first rune before returning it to the bag and casting again. Alternatively, pick three runes and cast them on the grid, letting them find their place on the grid, and repeat the process twice more. You may have to cast the last two or three runes individually.

Once the grid is full, read the runes in the following order from button to top. From the left: 1, 2, 3. From the right: 4, 5, 6. From the left: 7,8,9. You can read the rows as the events or main points of one continuous story. Alternatively, read the grid as a larger Norn reading with the first row for Urd, the past, the second row for Verdandi, the present, and the top row for Skald, the future. Another way to read the grid is to read it in sets of three, taking each row as a message. Sets of three can also be found vertically and diagonally. These messages can build on each other or indicate multiple factors at play.

THE RUNIC CALENDAR

For this reading we use the circle described on the rune cloth, or other surface. It should be fairly large with a clear area all around it. The circle can be sectioned into twelve sections like a clock. Each section represents a month.

Decide how you wish to continue the divination.

- Pick 12 runes like you did for the Norns and Grid readings and cast them as you would for the Grid reading, filling all the sections of the circle. Then, read the rune as influencing that month. Add the month's influences to get a broader picture. For example, Gebo falling in August or September could indicate a gift or exchanged gifts. In other words, an August wedding or proposal is likely or a favor is called in. It could also literally mean you receive an unexpected gift or that love goes well.

- Pick out the 12 runes that represent the months of the runic year. They are: Isa, Uruz, Berkano, Raidho, Perthro, Sowilo, Dagaz, Ger or Jera, Fehu, Ehwaz, Othala, and Hagalaz. Cast the runes in the way you feel is best, either individually or all at once. Apply the meaning of the rune and the message from its month to the qualities of the month on which the runes rest. This should give you unique messages for each divination. For example: Berkano in December could indicate the birth of a child or new idea, or the conception of one, during December. It could also mean new, fertile love is coming in for you in December. It could also mean that your mother visits in December, or that your creativity is inspired after a period of not creating much.

The Full Set and Circle Reading

This divination uses all the runes in a set and, depending on the cast, can require a lot of time.

Spread out the rune casting cloth and mix your runes well. When you're ready, you can empty your runes onto the circle in one go. You can also choose three runes at a time and cast them into the circle.

Read only the runes that fall inside the circle in the position and in relation to each other. If a rune is displaced by another, make a note of both, as it may be significant to the interpretation, showing what aspects are being replaced in the situation.

The Closing of the Divination

To close the divination, gather your runes and place them in their box or bag with respect. Fold away the casting cloth.

When you're ready, thank all the gods and beings you invoked at the start of the divination. Offer a gift to them in the form of a small offering such as a libation of liquor.

If you feel the need, return the hallowed space back to its original state by revoking your claim on it. This is especially good manners if you've done the reading outdoors in conserved or other natural regions.

Tips for Reading the Runes

- Listen to the runes. Your attunement should allow the flow of information between you and the rune.
- Blank runes are significant, as are the unmarked side of runes. If a rune lands blank side up in a casting, note the meaning of the rune. With it being or only showing its blank side, it indicates that those energies and influences are stable and not shifting soon, but still have bearing on the issue at hand. For example, Othala with its blank side showing could

indicate that the sale of your home may take a while longer, or that the issue around your family isn't going to shift soon.
- Look for runes in the same set falling close together. This can tell you if a situation can be changed by personal action or if it's fate and the will of the gods.
- Runes with similar themes or compatible themes may highlight an aspect that is central to the issue or that needs your attention first.
- Runes that fall outside a cast can be returned to the bag or box for the Norn and Grid readings, as well as the Calendar Divination.
- If you aren't getting any results from the reading (no readable runes in the circle) or you receive no messages from the rune or your intuition, it may not be the right time for a divination. Try again later that day or the next day. You may also want to cleanse your runes.
- If many runes are readable, but you feel there isn't a coherent message or you feel you aren't quite grasping all the elements they speak of, leave the cast as is for a few hours or overnight then take another look. You're sure to see the message clearly then.
- Intuition comes first. If you feel your intuition is contradicting the traditional meaning of the rune, it's usually better to let your intuition lead, unless there are other runes close by reinforcing the original meaning of the rune.
- If you find the same rune or runes appearing in all your casts, even if you're reading for someone else, that rune has an important message for you. Often when looking at that rune, your insight on a perplexing matter will suddenly become clear to you.
- Runes are smarter than you think. Rewording and recasting for a question you've just read on is most likely to give you the same result or a very sarcastic and obtuse one!

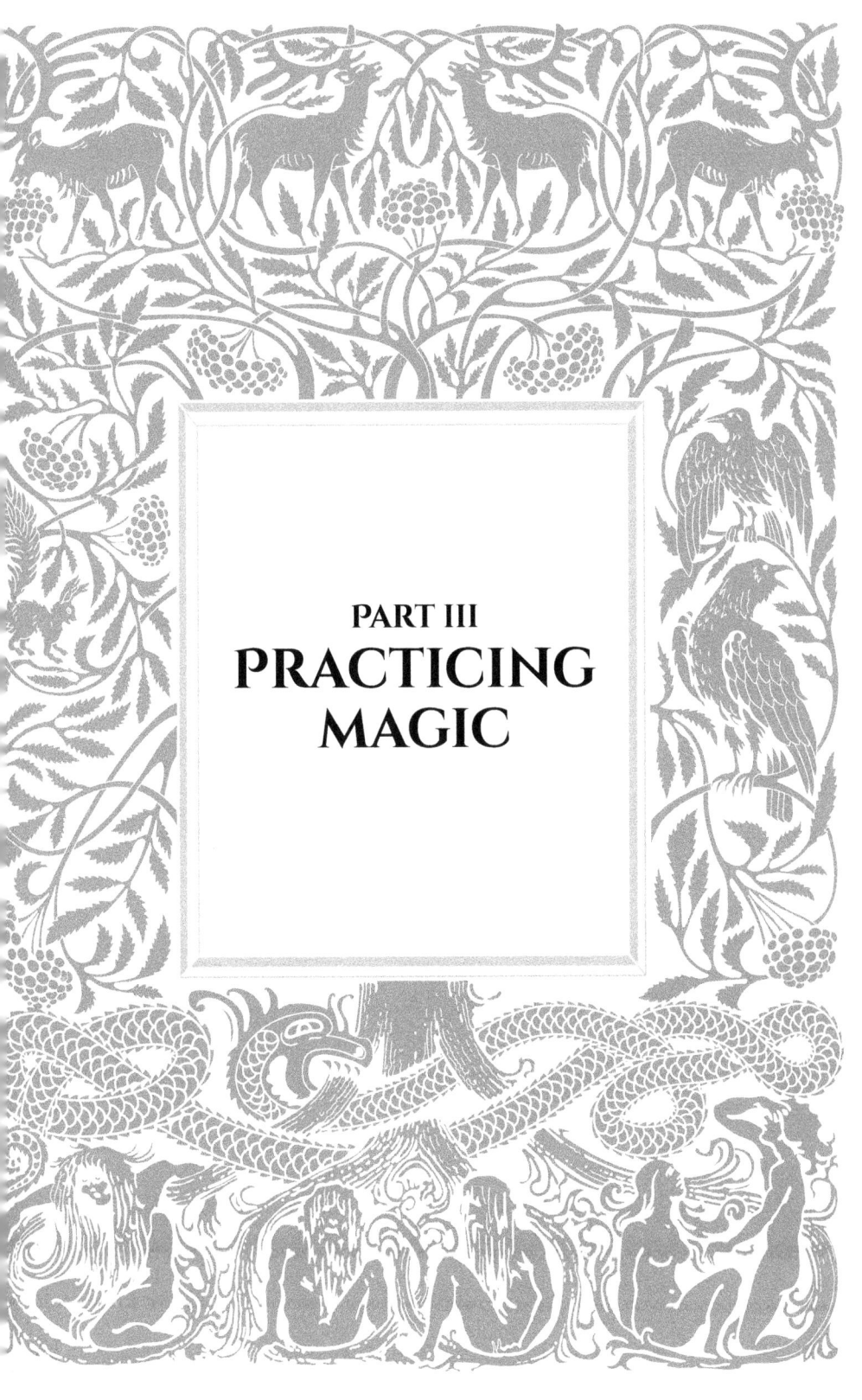

PART III
PRACTICING MAGIC

CHAPTER 8
PRACTICING SEIÐR

Seiðr, with its shamanismistic aspects, mainly focuses on the internal powers of the rune-master, *vitki*, or *völva*.

Most work and magic is done within—within their mental and spiritual bodies, and within other realms and dimensions that may not be physically accessible. Sometimes, seiðr practitioners may spiritually travel to "regions" and dimensions to talk to specific beings, gods, and ancestors.

Seiðr can therefore be seen as soul work, or spiritual and soul journeys. In what's known of the Norse traditions, the soul is regarded as various individual aspects. During magical battles, these aspects of the soul may be attacked—ancient remote warfare. By working with these aspects of the soul, shape-shifting may be possible. So, can people really shape-shift? Yes, but not in the way you think!

Seiðr is also used to draw things, people, and energy to you. It's believed that psychic threads were sent by practitioners and were used to draw to them the items and people they desired, were hired to obtain, or were needed by the community. Seiðr love spells probably used these methods to draw in lovers and wealth.

Since we know so little about seiðr, it's best to do your own research and follow your own inner guidance before attempting any seiðr practice. Before experimenting, no matter how short the experiment, always hallow the space. Never do seiðr work if you're tired or your energy and mood is low.

SOUL WORK OR HYGE-CRAFT

Little is known for sure what most Norse believed about the soul prior to the writings of Christian scribes, because before this the Norse didn't have the word "soul," or "sal," in their vocabulary. Even with the scribes' recordings, the entire concept of ancient Norse belief in the spiritual and non-physical aspects are likely to be incomplete or garbled to some extent. We do know that the soul may have been viewed in what we might think of as a fragmented or sectioned way. Foremost, in discussions of the soul with a Norseman or woman was the *hug*.

Hug

The *hug* is all that is intangible in a being—the mind, the appearance, the emotions, and even personality. It encompasses all the aspects of your soul. Your hug can stand apart from your physical aspects—like a double, even in another location. This may be the reason many Scottish folktales tell of a person's likeness being seen and interacting with people miles away from their dying physical body. The hug, however, is dependent on the physical body to survive, and perhaps vice-versa. It's believed that if you harm someone's hug, you physically harm that person. This is probably why remote magical battles were so intense and often determined the outcomes of the engagements. The *hug* is discernible by sensitive people and on the astral plane. It's there on the astral planes that hugs interact and perform seiðr and other forms of magic. The hug is also believed to retain aspects of your personality—traits that you carry and that help identify you on the astral plane.

Hyge

Also called *hidge* or *hugh*. According to Thorsson (1993) the hyge is the intellectual aspect of the soul, the part that thinks and is open to schooling. The *hyge* is logical, questioning, and carrying information. Huginn and Muginn, Odin's two ravens, are said to exemplify the hyge, corresponding to our understanding of the hemispheres of the brain.

Hyde

There's some debate about this aspect of the soul. Some say it's the physical aspects of the soul that determines a person's appearance. For others, the hyde is the astral body and psychic projects you can send. It's this part of the soul that's possible to transform into something that's different from your physical self; in other words, shape-shift. Naturally, it's not possible for a human form to twist and change into something it isn't. But the energetic or astral body is more malleable. It's said that if you do shape-shifting work or magic with a specific animal or your animal totem, then you'll slowly acquire some of the traits of that animal. Maybe this is why movies and books identify werewolves by their excessive hair.

Lyke

Also called *lich*, the physical, material part of the body; the vessel that holds the other aspects of the soul. The lyke is believed to merely be the vessel for the hug, and without the hug, lies lifeless. To the Norse, the lyke or body was as a housing for their soul. In order to live well and do strong magic, they had to have a fit and strong body. A Norse shaman was sure to train their body as well as mind, soul, and spirit.

Myne

Also called *mynd* or *minni*. The memory aspects of the soul that store experiences, knowledge, and even previous lifetimes.

Working with myne and healing memories could employ soul retrieval and past life exploration.

Wode

Wode is the part of a soul that binds everything together and is emotional. This is where inspiration and intuition stem from. Wode is said to be related to mood. Wode can also refer to the ease in which you can achieve bliss or a spiritual ascension through meditative and altered states of mind. In other words, it's the part of your soul most receptive to communication with the divine.

Ond and Odr

Ond is breath, spirit, or energy that animates. This gift of Odin brings to life not only the lyke but the hug, too. Some see ond as a mechanism that binds or connects the body to the soul.

Odr is divine consciousness; an ecstasy of experience that your inner divinity begins to assimilate and express.

Hamingjar

The *hamingjar* is said to be your luck or fortune. In certain instances it's transferable—good or bad. Hamingjar isn't always random luck, but also good fortune earned by selfless acts for your community. It can be transferred between a father and his heir and between a king and his subjects. Hamingjar can also mean spirit guardian—the one who accompanies you no matter your fate.

Godi/Gydja/Higher Self

The custom that anyone could act as a priest or priestess is because of the aspect of the soul that is your inner divinity, the godi and gydja—the god within you, also known as your higher self or the divine within you. The Norse religion can therefore be observed anywhere by anybody.

ABOUT PRACTICING SEIÐR

Seiðr is learned and practiced over a period of time. It takes dedication and perseverance to master the techniques that allow the vitki and völvur to discern the wyrd, weave it, sing it into being, shape-shift, and successfully protect or curse. In other words, don't expect to learn seiðr within a few weeks or even a few months. Traditionally, vitki trained for a minimum of three years.

Preparation for Practicing Seiðr

Three main considerations should be made before setting down the path of seiðr. One is to find a mentor or another who can watch over you while you're in a trance state, The other consideration is time and commitment, while the third consideration is safety and motivation.

Much of seiðr work involves being in trance or altered state while working or gathering information. If you get into trouble "on the other side," you want to have help on hand to help ward you and get yourself—your hug—back into your body. Besides the psychic vulnerabilities, there's also the physical ones as well. Having a partner is safer all round for both of you.

Becoming a seiðr worker is not something you can delve into lightly. It's best to talk to seiðr workers and to research for yourself as much as you can before embarking on this journey. Everyone's journey will be unique, and all will be testing, but it can be rewarding, too. Seiðr requires not just time, but commitment, too. You'll be experiencing some weird and mind-altering things. It will impact you irrevocably and you will change. You may find that you have a patron deity or that your work requires negotiation with gods, wights, and other magic beings. Are you prepared mentally and emotionally to deal with them for the rest of your life? Remember that "a gift for a gift" will always apply. Your allegiance and loyalty to your god or gods may be tested vigorously. Hindering or mischievous energies could also attack you, causing you to become elf-shot. This can lead to illness, particularly in your joints, or even cancer.

This brings us to safety and motivation. Why do you want to practice seiðr? Is the motivation worth the risks? Keep in mind that during seiðr work your physical body is vulnerable wherever it's laying. Your psychic self is also at risk, sometimes more so than your lyke. Your energetic self may be attacked or manipulated by wights, gods, and other energies. You may also get confused and lost while soul-walking, and may not be able to find your way back to your body. This can lead to a very real physical death.

When first practicing seiðr, always err on the side of caution. Find a partner or a group to work with. Take the safer approach until you've developed the skills and knowledge to get yourself out of trouble, or better yet, are steeped in the ways of avoiding it altogether. Then, too, remember that each journey—each working—is also within the hands of the Fates, and not just your own.

Methods of Practicing Seiðr

There's no hard and fast rule to practicing seiðr, but your practice should include one or more of the following elements:

- rhythmic sounds or a beat such as a drum beat or a chant
- going into a trance or other altered state
- being unconscious of your physical body

However, the very first step you should do in both your physical and energetic bodies is to ward yourself thoroughly and establish boundaries that need to be respected with any guides, gods, or wights you may deal with.

Wardings

To set up a ward is to set up an energetic or magical barrier to protect whatever is inside it. During seiðr and other magical work, this will be you—body, mind, and soul. Just as we hallow ground for blóts and rune divination, we can hallow the environment for seiðr work. However, state which beings and gods you'd like to work in so that they aren't filtered out by your ward. Incense and a cleansing smoke ceremony or saining can also be done.

The easiest way to set up a ward is to imagine a circle of golden or purple light around you. Remember to ward your energetic body, too.

Talismans, including runes and crystals, can also help ward you and your physical body. Additionally, a magic warding sign can be drawn on your forehead. Ensure all your personal wards resonate and respond to the programming of you and you alone. And also ensure that others present also have their personal wards up and running. Diana Paxson advises that you put up wards during each step of your journeying as well as asking your hamingjar and spirit guides for additional protection. (Paxson, 1993).

Rhythmic Chants

While galdr calls for rune galdrs to be intoned, seith requires chanting. This may not be the rune poems or runic rhythms, but invocations of the gods and melodious chanting. Some use medieval norse chants or songs, and others songs with a lullaby feel. The song should inducing you into a relaxed, trance-like, and receptive state. It's advised that if a chant or a song is used to lead the practitioner into a trance, that the same songs or singing be used to lead them out of it.

Trance

The trance state allows the seiðr worker's hug to leave their body and conduct the tasks they set out to do. A trance therefore needs to be carefully induced, maintained, and ended. While the chants and rhythms work to open the way, maintain it, and facilitate the work; sometimes more is needed to achieve the right degree of consciousness and facilities to conduct the seiðr goal.

Breathing techniques are probably the easiest to learn and use successfully. Use one that you feel comfortable with and which allows you to relax. One method employed is to breathe in for a count of three, hold for a count of three, exhale for a count of three, wait for a count of three. As you continue, extend the wait between the exhale and the next inhale to induce a light trance.

Natural substances are used by experienced practitioners to gain a suitable altered state. These can be plant or mineral-based with the seiðr worker studying and working with the plant beforehand. Care should be taken with the quantity consumed, and it's best to have someone watch over you if you're using this method to induce a trance.

Rhythm and ritual and sleep deprivation are other methods of inducing trance. Repetitive actions can bring relaxation to an individual while the monotony can induce a trance when you're literally "bored out of your mind." The repetitive action could be dancing, shaking or beating a musical instrument, chanting, and so forth. Rhythm in the form of a beat or drumming is effective in also carrying you through a journey to other realms. You can "ride" the rhythm to your astral destination and then back again, as the Norse rode their horses across the land and Odin rode Sleipnir through the realms.

Other methods to gain a suitable trance state include sacred sex, fasting, ordeals, and guided journeying.

- As you gain proficiency in falling into a trance easily and returning from them successfully and with little drama, it's time to practice focused attention.

- Controlling your mind through focused attention is what will make you strong on the astral plane and able to fulfill your tasks without losing your way.

- Learning and practicing focused attention is also the skill that will allow you to hold your hug in the shape you wish to travel in the astral plane, as well as to conduct spells and other magical actions according to your will.

You can practice focused attention for seiðr in the following way:

- Study an object, for example a pen. Note it's visual qualities. Close your eyes and visualize the pen. Practice until you have an accurate mirrored image when you visualize the pen.
- Pick up the pen. Feel its texture, its weight, and any other qualities that define it. Once you're confident you have all the aspects noted and memorized, put the pen down. Close your eyes, visualize the pen, then feel it in your hand.
- Finally, in your mind's eye, turn the pen around so you're viewing it in 3D and you're experiencing the pen as if you're holding it.
- Repeat the process with another object.

This skill will allow you to recreate your magical tools in the astral plane, if needed.

JOURNEYING

Journeying, also called sitting out or ùtiseta, is the second process for seiðr. Once you've mastered being in a trance state and are proficient in protecting yourself and being conscious in the astral plane. you are ready to move around the astral plane and interact with the energies there.

It's preferable to do your journeying outdoors in a safe area where it's unlikely you'll be disturbed. Carry with you a drinking vessel of choice, a drink you'll make offerings and libations with, and something with which you can sit comfortably on the ground. Once you arrive at your chosen spot, discern which direction is north. Arrange things so you're facing north and in a sitting position.

Find a method of accessing the astral plane that suits you. This may be visualizing a rune as a portal into its energies, a guided visualization of entering the otherworld, or going into a light trance and maintaining it until you feel you're no longer in your body or aware of your five senses.

When you're ready, you can call your fetch or seek out your allies in the astral realms. Your fetch—you may have more than more—is an aspect of your energy or a totem of yours. It can appear as a mirror of yourself in either gender (your fetch-husband or fetch-wife), an animal, or an abstract form.

It's important to seek or call your fetch the first time you go journeying. Identifying your fetch and building a relationship with them ensures you always have an ally and a helper in the astral realms. They'll also provide you with additional protection and security in the astral realms.

Calling Your Fetch

The following process is adapted from Thorsson (1993).

Sit for some time, composing a call to your fetch and waiting for the right moment. Your invocation to your fetch can be directed to an animal that you feel is your totem, or with which you've had previous communication or have confirmation of. If you aren't sure or don't yet have knowledge of your totem animal, you should compose a general call to your fetch. In your invocation, call and honor your fetch, letting them know that you seek a connection.

For example, an invocation could read something along the lines of:

Fetch of mine, I call to you with high regard. Show me yourself, your wisdom, and your power. I wish to learn from you, and you from me. Together, we will grow and be stronger.

You may choose to use a different tone, rhythm, or language. Call in the way that feels most authentic and right to you.

Once your call is done, it's time to make a boast (toast) to your fetch. Fill the cup with the drink and raise it high. Toast and honor your fetch.

An example of the a toast to your fetch could be along the lines of:

I praise and honor you, my holy fetch. You protect me. You educate me. You show me the way, and you aid me through difficulties. I honor and praise you, my true fetch and friend.

Then, drink half of the cup from the toast and pour the rest of the liquid on the ground in front of you. Keep the cup on your right-hand side.

Next, sing to your fetch. It can be one repeated sentence requesting your fetch to reveal itself. Imagine your fetch appearing in front of you. In time, your fetch will reveal itself. Sometimes, if you are in a suitable area, a real animal may appear to confirm the image in your mind's eye or, if you've not yet had it appear.

Now, talk to your fetch. Have a conversation with it. Enquire its name and anything else that would allow you to recognize your fetch from others that may look or sound like it. Ask if it is willing to work with you. What are the boundaries? This communication forms and strengthens the bond between you. Listen to your fetch if they have anything further to share with you, too.

Once the conversation is over, thank your fetch.

The next step before you conclude this journey is to call your fetch back to you and to internalize the bond. Simply saying something along the lines of: *Fetch/their name, come back!* Your fetch should return and remain in close proximity to you.

End this journey by stating something along the lines of: *And so the work is complete.* From now on, your fetch can be at your side in an instant. You can call on your fetch for help or conversation even when you aren't in a trance.

Thorsson further recommends blessing your fetch and its species if they are an animal within 24 hours.

Gaining More Allies and Further Journeying

One of the first things to do on your next journeying is to find your spirit allies or guides from one of the nine worlds. They, too, will help with protection in the astral planes and share knowledge that you seek. Paxson (1995) suggests seeking *álf* and *dís* allies in ancestral barrows and mounds or *hamingja*—spirit animal allies. Wights, and gods too, can also be spirit allies. If searching for allies among the gods and wights, always keep in mind the "gift for a gift" cardinal rule. Much like with your fetch, have a conversation with likely allies and learn how to discern that the ones you speak to are really the ones you're connected to, as sometimes the astral work can be deceptive. Ask what they need from you, and if they're willing to provide you with what you seek. It's an exchange—a barter—but one based on friendship and mutual regard rather than just commerce. Like with your fetch, you can communicate regularly with your spirit allies and *hamingja*, even when not in a trance.

Keep in mind that you should only attempt making spirit allies once you're well-versed in trance, in protection, and have your fetch to look out for you. You don't want to be a host to a possession because you didn't know the ropes.

A Note on Possession and Riding

The new *vitki* or *völva* unused to traveling in the astral plane must beware of spirits and gods who may trick you and possess your body, leaving you stranded in the astral plane.

If you have worked with a spirit ally or god for a while and trust them implicitly, you may consider sharing your body with them—hosting them temporarily. This is called "riding." If you want your body back, be sure to invoke a binding agreement of when your body will be returned to you, preferably in absolute time.

Vitkar and *völvur* are also said to have the ability to "ride" a person if they gain permission.

CHAPTER 9
PRACTICING SPÁ

As much of spá-craft involves foresight or prophecy, your innate psychic abilities determine how to approach spá-practice. If you already have a strong intuition and foresight about general matters, or find yourself helping others heal by intuition and remedies that tend to work, you are more than halfway to being a spákona or spá-madr. If you aren't yet strongly intuitive, you may still read another's orlog by interpreting the wyrd through trance and the assistance of your fetch and other spiritual allies. Then, too there are the incantations to heal and weave household magic which many folk can, and still do, use.

Spae-craft is less risky to your astral body as it generally doesn't involve journeying. Prophecy and information is gleaned by consulting with spirit allies and the gods and sharing what was said. In other words, it involves channeling messages.

While spaekonas were seen as practicing divination and prophesying using domestic and acceptable methods, they used methods similar to seiðr-workers and that are linked to their learning from Sámi shamans. These methods were employed to control the weather, call fish and animals to nets and bows, and practice energetic healing from a trance state. Spáe-craft also involves the brewing of potions and poisons for various spells and medical uses.

About Practicing Spá

Spákona and völvur may identify with the energy of Frigg and Freya, with Frigg being the stronger. Carrying a staff that may be an echo of the distaff and spindles used for spinning and weaving threads, spaekona specialize in sympathetic magic instead of direct engagement with a person's hug or soul aspects.

Like seiðr practitioners, spákona also utilize trances—usually light trances—singing or galdr, and shape-shifting or astral projections in animal form. And like seiðr-workers, spaekonas can also be fatally hurt if their astral projects or hugs are wounded.

Preparations for Practicing Spá

Preparations for practicing spá are much the same as seiðr. Even those who are already attuned and confident in their intuition and knowledge of the lore take years to fully understand the songs and galdr, the workings of wyrd, rules of working magic and countering spells, and the control of weather and calling of animals. Learning and study are an ongoing process for any völvur, even within a domestic context.

Spákona often learn from their mothers and grandmothers or an older spá-worker within the community with whom they may apprentice themselves if they have "the gift." Much of the knowledge is handed down orally. Most spáworkers practiced alone except for occasional meetings to address issues that went beyond their local districts.

With much of the information they shared produced through inner work, spákona often followed rituals to establish reliable open channels with spirit. Like the Norns, they read orlog, but do little to change it. They didn't interfere before an event, but treated those who lived through it. It's not advisable to undertake spá-work when tired or upset.

In preparation for any spá-work, no matter the size of the gathering, the area is hallowed, as are the tools. The spaekona also performs some ritual of purification. This may involve a similar singular ritual such as a visualization, or it could involve the use of salt and crystals or *saining*.

Methods for Practicing Spá

Spá-work is in its aspects of divining the orlog of a person, region, or even the world, and it is familiar to many students of the esoteric already. To prophesy, channels were opened. To divine a future, tools such as tarot, reading of the herbs, candle readings, and other divination methods were consulted.

In the Highlands of Scotland and Orkney, spaewives are well-known for their reading of tea-leaves. Naturally, the runes were consulted, too. The tools depend on the practitioner's preference. After all, the tools are not important, it's the quality of the channel that's opened.

The Light Trance

Almost all of spá-work begins by achieving a light-trance state. Breathwork may be used or mild herbal relaxants employed to get the spaekona into a receptive state. Once a great state of relaxation is achieved, protocols are established with the spae-workers' guides or fetch. Questions are asked once the wights are honored.

Spákona may also go spirit walking to discover an answer or information, or to speak to an ancestor or others who have passed away. As they receive information from the astral world, they speak it.

Once the channeling is done, care is taken to clear the energies, to cut the energetic ties that may have been established, and to ensure that the channel is closed. The hallowed ground, often found in their home or a community area, is returned to its original state.

Incantations and Charms

Incantations, also known as folk charms, were handed down from spaekona to the apprentices. This usually involved invoking a deity for help in healing or orlog divining. Often, for orlog divination, the Norns would be invoked. For protection, Thor would be called upon. For good crops, Frey or Njord would be invoked.

Njord and other air and sea spirits are invoked for charms involving the weather and abundance, while Tiw is invoked to help find justice.

While some incantations were muttered, many used galdr. Modern Wiccans practice these ancient and tailor-made incantations and galdr in their spellwork. Risting (drawing) of symbols and runes in the air above a person or a preparation of herbs and other remedies added to the potency of the charm.

The High Seat Ceremony

The grandest form of spae-craft was practiced in the community. During festivals, near temples, and during times of celebration or community stress, such as approaching war or the changing of the climate, the community would gather to hear the prophecies of the völvur or spaewife. This event was very different from the usual domestic setting of the spae-work and relied on great ceremony.

The völvur was offered a seat above all others, often situated on top of an ancestral mound where the ancestor buried there could help with the divining. On the seat was a cushion of feathers to further aid the journey of prophecy.

The spá-workers dress was also very different, appearing in full magical regalia with the distinctive blue cloak, cat fur hat and gloves, and her staff of office.

Below the high seat sat singers and spá or seiðr practitioners. Beyond them sat the rest of the community.

The ceremony began with the chanting and singing by the singers, calling in the helpers of the spáworker. The rhythm might have carried many on individual journeys but only the völvur would dance and speak.

When the völvur sensed the spirit allies were satisfied with the song, the prophesying would begin. This took the form of question and answer with the community asking and the völvur answering through the open channel. Once the prophecy was done, the singers sang the channel close. Afterwards, the community may have offered a sacrifice and eaten together.

For modern völvur and spaekonas, this ceremony may be practiced on a smaller scale, or an abbreviated form if the divination is conducted at home or in a small group.

Wand Work

While we know völvurs and spaekona held traditional staffs that may have evolved into wands, little is known about their actual use. What is known from reports on Sámi shamanism is that wands and staffs were used to draw in fish and animals towards the spaekona's community.

Others believe the wand or staff derive from the spindle and distaff used in spinning and weaving thread, linking the spáwork to that of the Norns. Besides reading the orlog, this theory also considers the spáworker a weaver of fate and does not quite sit well with the accepted beliefs in the Norns and the resilience of personal destiny and fate. However, some seiðr and spae-craft may have strived to "fix," or divert threads of fate temporarily for political reasons or personal gain. It's more likely that the spaekona and völvur traveled or followed threads to discern truly the interwoven and individual destinies of people.

At the burial of the spaekona or völvur, her staff or wand was bent so no others could use it.

Runes and Omen Reading

Spáwork also interprets omens or natural signs to determine outcomes and influences. Some of these observances are still around with us. Sayings such as, "Red sky at night, shepherds' delight. Red sky at dawn, shepherds mourn" still prove true today.

Birds remain significant omens, with ravens signifying Odin's influence at hand. Their behavior provided signs from war to Odin's favor. Eagles spoke of warriors, courage, and Odin's presence. Cormorants with wings set to enclose someone were signs of protection through nearby troubles.

Plants also carried omens. Strawberries were the fruit of Freya. Love or Freya herself is around.

Then, too, there were the weather and season omens…

CHAPTER 10
CREATING GALDR STAVES

Galdr or galdor is a magic incantation used by vitkar and völvur for various magical tasks. In the making of a personal rune set, the singing and chanting to activate the rune is galdr magic.

Galdr staves are also known as "taufr," or a talisman. They often contain bind runes or a spell written on a natural substance. Galdr staves were probably first carved on wood, stone, or bone. Later, they were carved on metals and even lead. Today, paper and ink are often used, too.

Much of the magic signs and helms of awe that we know and use today comes from an Icelandic grimoire, Galdrabòk, written around the 17th century C.E.

About Creating Galdr and Rune Spells

Rune spells have two parts: the written or engraved symbols, and the galdr or incantation.

There's some debate about whether galdr and rune songs were in fact sung or spoken, if they had words, or if the melody was most important and words unnecessary. Some references suggest that galdr songs and verses were sung in a high register to imitate birds of prey. Other sources suggest the incantations were spoken, though some parts of it may have been under the singer's breath, "keeping part of the song for himself" as the Finnish shamans did. (Siikala, 1990).

Galdr songs were often not shared with other practitioners, partly to retain the power of the song to the singer, and partly to prevent others abusing the magic. This can be seen in the *Hávamál* when Odin speaks of the rune spells he knows, but does not share the galdr or words.

Galdr can be either a mantra, or a poem or rhyme using alliteration. Kennings, or common references to a subject such as sif's hair for gold, appear in galdr incantations.

Resonance is favored when practicing galdr, with sounds drawn from deep in your diaphragm and felt within your body, especially for the vowel sounds.

Before you write your own, it's a good idea to study the rune poems and Norse poetry such as the Hávamál and the Eddas to learn the cadences of the poems before you emulate them.

You may also want to study old Norse kennings if you wish your personal galdrs to be very traditional.

As you practice, you're likely to build a tool box of galdrs to sing. While this is good news, some spells may need you to create unique galdrs. This has the benefit (or the downside) of you being the sole owner of the galdr and its power.

Some of the most powerful galdr contain riddles as well the poetry.

Deep in the ocean swims the many-teeth.
Not a bite it eats.
Waters of mysterious calm,
Keep it from harm.

One of the best known healing galdrs is from the story of Odin healing Baldur's lame horse. It survived in Orkney in the local dialect as the "Wreestin' Thread."

The most powerful healing lines were also preserved in various known galdrs used by spaekonas. The words are to the effect of:

*Bone to bone, Blood to blood
and limb to limb, like they were glued.*
(Merseberg Incantations via Sigurd Towrie, Orkney Saga)

PREPARATION FOR CREATING GALDR STAVES OR TAUFR

Before you begin, it's recommended to plan or sketch your bind rune or sigil. A pencil and paper would be best for this. Decide on the material you wish to rist your rune on. If you're aren't sure, consider where and how you'll deploy your rune spell or talisman. If it's a short-term spell or task, paper or cardboard may serve well. If the bind rune is to protect a vehicle, a wooden or metal disc may work well. And if the bind rune is to ward land, then a stone tablet or marker may be best.

Composing your galdr before you begin singing will help you concentrate on building the rhyme and resonance instead of freestyling with the sounds and words. Remember that the most powerful spells sung were melodious.

Gather the tools, material, and equipment you'll need to create the spell or talisman. Runes and runic talismans were often finished by rubbing blood or spit across them. Alcohol was also used. Fortunately, a red paint or marker is acceptable to activate rune or rune spells. You may also want to include a ruler and protractor to get the lines neat and straight.

Set aside sufficient time to go through the entire process. Ensure you're in good health and rested before you begin.

In addition, you may prepare yourself as you did when making your personal set of runes. This includes hallowing the space you're working in. It wouldn't do to create the rune that inadvertently brings us closer to Ragnarok!

Methods for Creating Galdr Signs and Talismans

Bind runes, talismans such as Helms of Awe, magical staves, and magical signs and formulae all have similar processes to work through.

Bind Runes

Bind runes are formed when two or more runes are combined into a single symbol to act as a spell or a talisman. Worn as a piece of jewelry or placed significantly on or near the object it's meant to work on, the bind rune's magic will permeate through and have an effect.

Bind rune designs can be arranged in any way you find pleasing or "right." This can be a line of runes appearing like a sentence, or the arrangement of the runes into a graphic. The designs can run vertically, horizontally, or in a circle using staves crossing or meeting at the center.

Because of the nature of runes lines, combining two or more runes can also result in many more runes forming within the design. A good example is the Bluetooth symbol that combines Kenaz ᚲ and Beorc ᛒ. With Kenaz on the main line facing left and Berkano facing right on the main line, multiple runes are formed in this bind rune. Gebo, Perthro, Sowilo, Laguz, and Hagalaz can all be seen as well. It's important to be aware of all the runes visible and hidden in a bind rune as this will have an effect on the results produced by the rune. Therefore, planning your bind rune before you rister it and sing it into being is vitally important!

Whether you're working a rune spell or creating a talisman, the following process is one of the best starting points.

- Contemplate on your sigil or rune spell purpose beforehand.
- Once you've broken down your spell's components, select your runes to use. For example, if it is a healing talisman for someone suffering from sinusitis, you may consider using laguz, tiwaz, uruz, thorn, and wunjo.

- Allow your creativity to flow as you try out various combinations and designs.
- When you've found the design that looks and feels right to you, search the design for hidden runes. If a hidden rune feels like it's weakening the bind rune, you may want to redesign to avoid forming that rune. If this happens pay attention to the meaning of the rune. It may have some significance in what you're aiming to achieve.
- When you're comfortable with your bind rune with its visible and hidden runes, you're ready to begin making your bind rune or talisman.
- Prepare the surface you're etching your runes onto, or select the color of board and paper if you're inking your rune spell. White is often best, but if you'd like you can match the color of the board to the talisman's purpose. For example, if your bind rune is to help you strengthen your magic, you may want to use blue board or blue paper.
- When you and your materials are ready, begin carving or writing the runes, tracing them individually on the design even if it means going over certain lines again. Take your time, singing each rune's galdr and any rune spell you may have prepared. Alternatively, you can sing your runespell once you're all done. Continue to contemplate the purpose of the bind rune and the effect you wish it to have.
- Once you're done, sit for a little while with your bind rune. Think again of the individual runes that form it and their purpose in the goal you're aiming to achieve. If you haven't sung your rune spell yet or wish to sing it again, do so now.
- When you feel it's time to close the process, set your bind rune aside and give thanks in a small blót to the gods.
- Unhallow the space.
- Place your bind rune where it will have the most effect and allow its power to take you to your goal.

HELMS OF AWE

The helm of awe is a powerful runic symbol said to empower the wearer and incapacitate the wearer's enemies and opponents. Called the æglshjálmar, or helmet of awe, Thorsson describes these as symbolic maps of the universe along which serpent power or other magic travels.

Helms of awe, also known as the helms of terror, are said to be unreadable by those who don't have the key to decode them so ensuring the æglshjálmar would be hard to counter magically.

In its simplest form, a helm of awe resembles the familiar pictograph of a snowflake drawn by children with two equal lines crossing at the center, their endings bisecting v-shaped marks with lines of equal length.

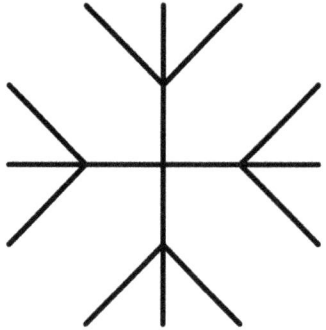

Drawn on square surfaces, the sign is divided into three concentric rings. The inner ring represents the core—the wearers essence. The middle ring symbolizes the inner universe of the wearer—their spiritual and psychic experiences. The outermost circle encapsulates the whole of the outer or physical universe. Runic elements are placed along the different arms of the helm along with signs controlling the flow of energy. In effect, a helm of awe is the magical equivalent to an electric circuit board, even going so far as to use similar circular and bracketed signs to signal terminal endings and the return of energy!

A helm of awe works by streaming magic from the core of the vitki, concentrating and directing it in specific ways, then projecting it out into the outer universe and their opponents. Power can also be returned to the vitki through certain arms, so conserving their power simultaneously.

Casting a helm of awe follows much of the same process as creating a bind rune. The differences lie in that the helm of awe and other magic signs can have more stylized runes and curved lines. The following symbols can be used at the end of lines to direct and redirect the flow of magical energy:

- ᚤ and ᚩ flows out into the ring or zone
- ᛁ and ᛁ returns to the line or core
- ᛘ is split and directed outwards

Other symbols, curved and straight, can also be used to direct energy through the helm and so through the universe.

Runes can also be stylized by introducing or substituting curves. As long as the vitki's intention is strong throughout the casting and when in use, the magic of the helm will remain powerful.

Helms of awe could also be drawn on the forehead of a warrior or vitki before going into battle using spit.

Magical Signs and Formulae

Vitkis, spákonas, and runemasters also use magical signs and formulae called *galdramyndir* to cast and use as part of their magical tools. Although these signs don't stem from runes, they are noted in Icelandic galdor-books and produced with the same processes used for bind runes and helms of awe.

These galdr signs are more formulaic and may be even more ancient than bind runes. Specific signs and formulae are cast for specific needs. Many of their components such as the curved terminal endings resemble aspects of the helms of awe.

Here a few examples:

The *Kaupaloki*, or dear closer, is a type of galdramyndir used during business deals to make successful conclusion.

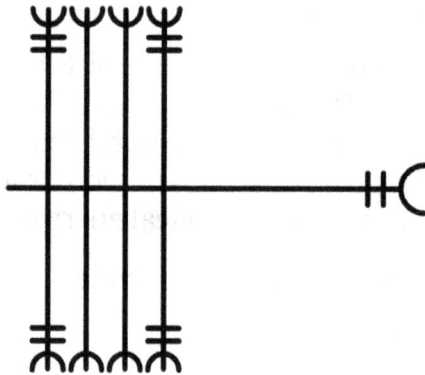

The Thiofastafur is a type of galdramyndir used to discover a person's identity that might have stolen something from you.

MAGICAL STAVES

Galdrastafur, or magical staves, are another Icelandic contribution to the Norse galdr. Their nature is to conceal the presence and workings of magical information and names as well as bind runes.

These magical staves begin as bind runes, are modified by the vitki or spaekonas will and creativity, then enhanced further into a work of art and magical symbol. These are also called sigils and are fairly easy to create if you're already familiar with bind runes.

For instance, the original binding rune looked something like this:

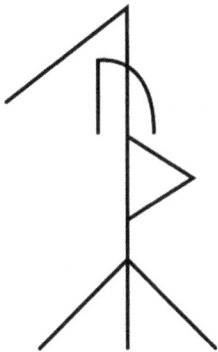

It was then re-worked into this form:

To create a magical stave, follow the first steps of the process used in creating bind runes. Instead of choosing your runes, write out the word or the name in the runic alphabet. These will be your runes used to create the bind rune.

Next, create your bind rune. Once you are satisfied with your bind rune, it's time to allow your creative inspiration to flow. Modify the lines of the bind rune however you wish. The power and working of this magical stave comes from your will and intention, simultaneously planting itself in your subconscious and the magical stave.

Feel free to mirror runes and transform straight lines into curves, although the central line is usually kept straight, the modifications occurring along its length. Angles of lines may also be changed. Try to aim for fluidity and symmetry with the forms. All the while, sing your galdr and visualize the symbol working its power through the universe.

Once you're satisfied with your magical stave's appearance, you're ready to activate it. First visualize the energy flowing through the stave from the center outwards. Then make a statement of the purpose of the rune and your intent in using it. Once you're done, invoke the gods, then end with something to the effect of: *So mote it be*.

Your magical stave is now ready to hang as decor, a plaque, or placed somewhere you wish to influence.

CONCLUSION

It seems that though the Norse gods did fade out like a temporary religious Ragnarok, Yggsdrasil and us humans are still in need of their wisdom and support—or maybe it's the other way round. Whichever is true, the branches of Norse magic are reaching further out of obscurity and into greater prominence, joining the diversity of beliefs and practices that make Midgard so special.

Thor and Odin never really faded away nor did they go to sleep. Thor held fast to his lands and popularity by being true to his nature and protecting those around him. Even in the ages far removed from the culture that conceived him, his absolute dependability and steadfastness (or is it stubbornness?) make him the god everyone likes or calls on anyway because he gets the job done.

Odin shape-shifted or donned his disguise, playing bit parts in other pantheons and remaining in the hearts of those who sought knowledge always, new ways to amuse, new ways to be, and a love and connection to the Earth Mother. With his return, he'll share new and old knowledge and maybe keep us hanging for his amusement and to teach us that our power lies within.

Frigg also hid in plain sight, healing, spinning orlog with the spaewives and weaving new ones for these new times with every home divination. Together with The Norns, she is as much a part of the Wyrd as life itself. We see her as Odin's wife, as Baldur's mother, as the matriarch and hostess who always keeps things in good order…Yet, she remains as mysterious as she ever was; the All Mother who holds sovereignty without question, yet yields to tradition when needed to.

Freya's never been one for the shadows. She found a new tribe in the wild men and wild women, with the so-called witchfolk, and their familiar traditions. Her flying chariot and black cats may have been traded for a broom, but after the witch trials and the invention of radar, who can blame her. At least, she's still having her feasts and fun. She's proven you can't put a good Vanir down.

Loki has spun himself into superstar status, remarketing himself as a younger version and the bad boy everyone loves, but he has the habit of tripping himself up or getting tied down. We have still to see if he's truly learned any new tricks. Still, the lessons he teaches us, the tricks he plays to make us laugh, may yet win him the place as the top dog of the Æsir—if Fenris and Thor don't take it away from him first.

The other gods may not have endured or adapted as well, but it does seem they may be returning to support the Earth Mother, to redress the balance, to offer gifts when the wyrd prompts them to; certainly, we're learning about Njord, Ullr, Skadi, and Sunna to name but a few, and how they can heal and prosper where we thought there was no hope. After all, they've lived through such times before.

The rediscovery and reinvention of Norse magic and traditions continue, too. A wealth of new discoveries from howes, ship burials, and new translations and evaluation of texts broadens our understanding of the complexities that make up seiðr, and the ceremonies and galdr that's used in spá. The more we learn, the more we realize we have to relearn, reassess, and review in our views of the lore and attitude to the gods and their true needs from us.

Spá and seiðr—the same but different—an analogy of the diversity that's been ignored and the marginalization or demonization of what we don't understand or would like to neatly label because we like the quick and easy and spá and seiðr takes time and commitment. How appropriate that the Norse have given us magic systems and practices that echo our society and signals how we can move out of apathy into living richer lives in the little give on the thread that the Norns have woven for us.

Gratitude must be given to those rune-master, shaman, spáworkers, faithful chroniclers, academics, and scribes who practiced despite terrible ostracization and persecution, or ridicule and damage to their reputations. They've given us a body of lore to reconstruct a way of life that is more harmonious to our planet, and maybe closer to our human natures than the perfection and restrictions demanded by other practices. All we have to do is consider whether the Norse way is our path or not.

While you may now be drawn into debates about seiðr vs spá, or how galdr should be sung—maybe even if joining an Asatrú congregation is the way forward or if you prefer being a vitka or völva in solitude—remember that Odin is still seeking wisdom and trying different ways to see what suits him best.

And while you may also be drawn into debates about whether Odin and his table of gods were real people or embodiments of energies and permissions our ancestors needed, remember that energy is real and ancient ancestors might have been gods in the eyes of the people they met.

Most of all remember:

- "A gift for a gift."
- Orlog is set but there is give in the thread.
- Don't judge the customs and culture of the ancestors by modern standards. You won't learn much that way.

Most of all, be cautious with those that aren't your allies, respect lone travelers, and be mindful of fate and consequences.
And finally, enjoy the humor of the Norse gods, Norse magic, and the Wyrd.

QUICK GUIDE TO RUNES

THE ELDER FUTHARK QUICK GUIDE

ᚠ	Fehu weath/cattle	f galdr sound
ᚢ	Uruz aurochs/vitality	u with galdr sound 'oo'
ᚦ	Thorn/giant	th with galdr sound 'th'
ᚨ	Ansuz	a with galdr sound 'ah'
ᚱ	Raidho	r with galdr sound 'rr'
ᚲ	Kenaz	k with galdr sound 'ke'
ᚷ	Gebo	g with galdr sound 'geh'
ᚹ	Wunjo	w with galdr sound 'w'
ᚺ	Hagalaz	h with galdr sound 'ha'
ᚾ	Naudhiz	n with galdr sound 'nor'
ᛁ	Isa	i with galdr sound 'is'
ᛃ	Jera	j or y with galdr sound 'jer'
ᛇ	Eiwaz	i with galdr sound 'ee'
ᛈ	Perthro	p with galdr sound 'per'
ᛉ	Elhaz	with galdr sound 'el'
ᛊ	Sowilo	s with galdr sound 'ss', 'zz', 'so'
ᛏ	Tiwaz	t with galdr sound 'te', 'ti'
ᛒ	Berkano	b with galdr sound 'beh'
ᛖ	Ehwaz	E with galdr sound 'eh'
ᛗ	Mannaz	m with galdr sound 'm', 'ma'
ᛚ	Laguz	l with galdr sound 'la'
ᛜ	Ingwaz	ng with galdr sound 'ng', 'ing'
ᛞ	Dagaz	d with galdr sound 'der', 'da'
ᛟ	Othala	o with galdr sound 'o', 'ot'

The Younger Futhark Quick Guide

ᚠ	fé cattle/wealth	f with galdr sound 'feh'
ᚢ	ùr auroch/strength	u, y, o with galdr sound 'oo', 'yirr', 'v'
ᚦ	thurs thorn/protection	th, dh with galdr sound 'th/ter'
ᚬ	áss god/inspiration	a with galdr sound 'ah'
ᚱ	reidh journey/ride	r with 're' or 'irr'
ᚴ	kaun fire	klg, ng with galdr sound 'ka'
ᚼ	hagall hail	h with galdr sound 'ha'
ᚾ	naudh need	n with galdr sound 'n'
ᛁ	íss ice/frozen	i, e, j with galdr sound 'ee', 'eye', 'ye'
ᛅ	ár harvest	a with galdr sound 'ah'
ᛋ	sigel sun	s with galdr sound 'ss', 'si'
ᛏ	Týr sky god/loyalty	t, d, nd with galdr sound 'te'
ᛒ	bjarkan birth	b, p, mb with galdr sound 'ber', 'per', 'mmb'
ᛘ	madhr man/tribe	m with galdr sound 'mm'
ᛚ	lögr water/feminine	l with galdr sound 'la', 'law'
ᛦ	ýr yew/protection/life/death	r with galdr sound 'ir', 'yirr'

THE RUNIC YEAR

ᛁ	Isa	January	Snow Moon
ᚢ	Ur	February	Horn Moon
ᛒ	Beorc	March	Mother Moon
ᚱ	Raidho	April	Cuckoo Moon
ᛈ	Perthro	May	Merry Moon
ᛋ	Sowilo	June	Sun Moon
ᛞ	Dagaz	July	Hay Moon
ᛜ	Ingwaz	August	Harvest Moon
ᚠ	Fehu	September	Wood Moon
ᛖ	Ehwaz	October	Hunting Moon
ᛟ	Othala	November	Fog Moon
ᚺ	Hagalaz	December	Wolf Moon

QUICK GUIDE TO POPULAR NORSE GODS AND GODDESSES

ODIN: THE ALL-FATHER, LORD OF THE WOLVES, THE HIDDEN ONE
- Æsir
- **Symbols:** blackthorn staff, the wolf, ravens, nine, eagle, horse, serpent, the spear
- **Day:** Wednesday shared with Mercury
- **Invoke him for:** seiðr, rune work, galdr, journeying, knowledge, advice in conflict, inspiration, invention, love galdr, blessing contracts, hallowing, hygge-craft

FRIGG: THE ALL-MOTHER
- Æsir
- **Symbols:** torc, bracelets, long hair, the sow, falcon or osprey
- **Day:** Friday shared with Venus
- **Invoke her for:** spa, domestic matter, divination, love and relationships, harmony, healing, family matters, manifesting new paths, blessing children and mothers, hallowing, sovereignty

FREYA: THE LADY, THE GIVER, GODDESS OF LOVE AND BEAUTY
- Vanir
- **Symbols:** black cats, a chariot drawn by black cats, the sow, the falcon
- **Day:** Monday shared with the Moon
- **Invoke her for:** seiðr, spa, erotic love, flight, fertility, galdr, journeying, business matters, crossing over, hallowing

Tiw: The God of Law, God of Courage, God of War and Peace, Spirit Warrior
- Æsir
- **Symbols:** oath rings
- **Day:** Tuesday shared with Mars
- **Invoke him for:** justice, courage, faithfulness, contracts, seeking peace and end to conflict, protection, winning a battle, hallowing

Ullr: God of Winter and Snow, The Hunter God, The God with the Skis
- Ancient
- **Symbols:** skis, bow, shield
- **Invoke him for:** seiðr, journeying, hallowing, success in hunts and searches, winter and other sport, weather magic, sovereignty, combat and survival issues

Frey: Lord of Prosperity, God of Plenty
- Vanir
- **Symbols:** horses, boar, deer/stag, a chariot pulled by a boar, a golden boar
- **Invoke him for:** seiðr peace, material things, physical passion, physical health, the land, blótsss, fertility

Thor: The Thunder God, The Thunderer
- Æsir
- **Symbols:** Hammer, thunderbolt, goat, lightning, belt, iron gloves
- **Day:** Thursday shared with Jupiter
- **Invoke him for:** hallowing, blótsss, redes, witnessing, protection, avenging, agriculture matters, physical strength, protection, land disputes

Baldur: God of Summer, God of the Sun, God of Spring
- Æsir
- Symbols: mistletoe
- Day: Sunday shared with the sun and Sunna
- Invoke him for: spa, blessings and blótsss, regeneration,

healing, beautifying, purifying, popularity

Loki: The Trickster, The Shape Changer
- Æsir
- **Symbols:** Double-horned helmet, mistletoe, entwined serpents

Njord: The Wealthy, The Ruler of Men, God of the Seafarers
- Vanir
- **Symbols:** ships, metal objects
- **Invoke him for:** spa, seiðr, abundance, prosperity, the sea, peace, diplomacy, counseling in love, divorce, rune work concerning wealth and career

The Norns: The Fates
- **Symbols:** the wyrd rune, the loom, thread
- **Day:** Saturday shared with Saturn
- **Invoke them for:** divination, hygge-work, galdr, spae-craft, rune work, prophecy, healing via disconnecting and de-cording

Sunna/Sol: Mistress of the Sun, Bright Bride
- **Symbols:** golden chariot, horses, gold and yellow items, stone
- **Day:** Sunday shared with Baldr and the sun
- **Invoke her for:** spae-craft, weather, crops, wealth, vitality, conception and continuity, journeying, at summer solstices.

Nerthus: Earth Mother, Great Mother
- **Symbols:** cart, landships
- **Invoke her for:** spá work, motherhood and mothering issues, during nature disasters, fertility, peace, purity, secrecy, blessings

Ing
- **Symbols:** cart, landships
- **Invoke him for:** spa, land issues, fertility

GLOSSARY

aett: a set of

álf: Scandinavian light elf, allies to the Æsir

Asatrú/Asatro: the Norse religion and its observances

boast: a toast in honor of someone or something

blóts: a blessing, a prayer, a religious ritual, or a thanksgiving to the gods and goddesses

casting runes: to throw or draw so you get random responses

casting signs: to draw and empower

dís: a female ancestor

fetch: an aspect of yourself on the astral plane or a spirit ally who'll always be with you

flything: trading insults

galdramyndir: a formulaic galdr sign used by spaewives

galdrastafur: galdr sign. A magical sigil originally derived from the runes

Gode: priest of a blótss

Gydje: priestess of a blótss

hallow: to claim a consecrated through rites of cleansing

hamingja: spirit animals in the astral plane, a spirit ally

hex-sign: Pennsylvania Dutch magic sign or sigil

hof: a sacred building such as a church or temple

jarl: Norwegian earl or son of a chieftain

journeying: travel in the astral plane and interactions there.

Jötnar: elementals and giants—the third tribe of god-like beings. **Jötunn**, singular

kenning: using a common description or substitute to refer to a thing or person

lot-cup: a random choice

magnate: a wealthy merchant or noble who owned much land

orlog: an person's destiny as laid down at birth by the Norns

rister: to draw, write, carve, and etch runes

runemaster: one who's mastered the runes and the making of magic signs and staves

saining: bathing and purifying with smoke from sacred or magical substances such as herbs or juniper

seith or seidh: seiðr

spae: spa

spaewives/spae-men: fortune-tellers, wise folk in the area, healers

spaekona/spaekona: spaewife

staves: shaved twigs, wooden sticks on which runes were engraved. An engraved runic message.

taufr: galdr staves or rune spells

things: official meetings to discuss and decide on judicial, land, and other matters of state. Also a parliament of sorts.

troth: faithful, loyalty, sworn to, a binding promise.
The Troth: The Way

vier/vi: hallowed land or a shrine

vitki: a male magic-worker or wizard. **Vitkar**: plural of *vitki*

völva/völvur: female prophetess/es and spa-workers

wyrd/weird: the web of the universe and the interconnectedness of everything.

REFERENCES

About Us – *Hrafnar*. (n.d.). Hrafnar.org. Retrieved February 1, 2022, from https://hrafnar.org/about-us/

Alexander, C. (n.d.). *Berries as symbols and in folklore*. https://cpb-us-e1.wpmucdn.com/blogs.cornell.edu/dist/0/7265/files/2016/12/berryfolklore-2ljzt0q.pdf

Ana. (2020, October 8). *Rune Magic 101*: What are and how to make bind runes | Time Nomads. Time Nomads | Your Pagan Store Online. https://www.timenomads.com/rune-magic-101-what-are-and-how-to-make-norse-bind-runes/

Anderson, R. B. (n.d.). *Norse mythology; or, The religion of our forefathers, containing all the myths of the Eddas, systematized and interpreted. With an introd., vocabulary and index*. S. C. GRIGGS AND COMPANY. https://www.gutenberg.org/files/65910/65910-h/65910-h.htm (Original work published 1876)

Anonymous. (n.d.). *Rune poems*. Wikisource. Retrieved February 5, 2022, from https://en.wikisource.org/wiki/Rune_poems

Axlund, P. (2021, February 4). *Smudging Ritual*. I Am EarthBound. https://iamearthbound.com/blogs/news/juniper-smudging-ritual

Balder – loved by everyone | The Swedish History Museum. (n.d.). Historiska.se. https://historiska.se/norse-mythology/balder-en/

Bl. (2020, November 10). Wikipedia. https://en.wikipedia.org/wiki/Bl

Blot. (n.d.). The-Asatrú-Community. https://www.theasatrucommunity.org/blótss

Eason, C. (1998). *The complete book of divination : how to use the most popular methods of fortune telling*. Piatkus.

Eason, C. (2002). *Ancient wisdom*. Parragon.

Edred Thorsson. (1993). *Northern magic: mysteries of the Norse, Germans & English*. Llewellyn Worldwide.

Freyasdaughter, C. (2016, September 7). *Offerings for the Gods, Part 3: The Jötnar*. Huginn's Heathen Hof. http://www.heathenhof.com/offerings-for-the-gods-part-3-the-Jötnar/

Galdr. (2021, June 11). Wikipedia. https://en.wikipedia.org/wiki/Galdr

Gundarsson, K. (n.d.). *Spae-Craft, Seiðr, and Shamanism – Hrafnar.* Hrafnar.org. Retrieved February 2, 2022, from https://hrafnar.org/articles/kveldulf/spaecraft/

Heidi. (2021, July 26). *Smoke Cleansing Around the World.* Blog. mountainroseherbs.com. https://blog.mountainroseherbs.com/smoke-cleansing

Helgason, M. S. (2015, July 15). *Heathens against hate: Exclusive interview with the high priest of the Icelandic Pagan Association.* Icelandmag. https://icelandmag.is/article/heathens-against-hate-exclusive-interview-high-priest-icelandic-pagan-association

Howard, M. (1980). *The magic of the runes : their origins and occult power.* Aquarian Press.

how to cleanse runes. (2012, October 22). Allegheny Candles' Blog. https://alleghenycandles.wordpress.com/tag/how-to-cleanse-runes/

Jay, N. (2020, October 15). *Loki – Norse God of Mischief.* Symbol Sage. https://symbolsage.com/loki-norse-god-of-mischief/

Joe, J. (n.d.). *Nerthus: Goddess of Peace and Prosperity.* Timeless Myths. Retrieved February 3, 2022, from https://www.timelessmyths.com/gods/norse/nerthus/

Kaldera, R. (2006). *Northern Tradition Shamanism: The Soul Map: A Northern-Tradition Shamanic Divination Method.* Www.northernshamanism.org. https://www.northernshamanism.org/soul-map.html

Kaldera, R. (2011). *Northern Tradition Paganism: What is Rökkatru?* Www.northernpaganism.org. https://www.northernpaganism.org/rokkatru/what-is-rokkatru.html

Kaushik, N. (2011, October 24). *Difference Between Norse and Viking | Difference Between.* Differencesbetween.net; Difference Between. http://www.differencebetween.net/miscellaneous/culture-miscellaneous/difference-between-norse-and-viking/

Kornevall, A. (2021, February 3). *Unearthing Ancient Magic in The Runes –Messages with Hidden Symbols and Powerful Numbers.* Www.ancient-Origins.net. https://www.ancient-origins.net/opinion-guest-authors/unearthing-ancient-magic-runes-messages-hidden-symbols-and-powerful-numbers-021193

Krasskova, G. (2011). *Nerthus's Shrine: Who is Nerthus?* Www.northernpaganism.org. http://www.northernpaganism.org/shrines/nerthus/about.html

Krasskova, G. (n.d.). *The Northern Sky : Praising Sunna*. Www. northernpaganism.org. Retrieved February 1, 2022, from https://www.northernpaganism.org/shrines/northernsky/sunna/praising-sunna.html

Lind, T. (2018, October 21). *Birds and their meaning in Nordic Folklore*. Tales from the Fairies. https://talesfromthefairies.wordpress.com/2018/10/21/birds-and-their-meaning-in-nordic-folklore/

List of gods and goddesses. (2021, October 26). Wikipedia. https://simple.wikipedia.org/wiki/List_of_gods_and_goddesses

Louis-Jensen, J. (n.d.). *The Norwegian Runic Poem as a Mnemonic Device The pictographic principle*. Retrieved February 5, 2022, from https://www.khm.uio.no/english/research/publications/7th-symposium-preprints/documents/louis-jensen.pdf

Mani. (2019, January 16). *Guldr Real Rune Magick*. Máni - the Norse Witch. https://theheart756621753.wordpress.com/guldr-real-rune-magick/

Mark, J. J. (2018, January 29). *Vikings*. World History Encyclopedia. https://www.worldhistory.org/Vikings/

McCoy, D. (n.d.). *Ullr*. Norse Mythology for Smart People. https://norse-mythology.org/ullr/

McKay, A. (2018, December 14). *Gods in Norse Mythology*. Life in Norway. https://www.lifeinnorway.net/norse-gods/

Mohnkern, S. (2009, April 16). *Introduction to Bind Runes | The Modern Heathen*. Http://Www.modernheathen.com; The Modern Heathen-Scott Mohnkern. http://www.modernheathen.com/2009/04/16/introduction-to-rune-staves/

National Museum Denmark. (2019a). *Human sacrifices? - National Museum of Denmark*. National Museum of Denmark. https://en.natmus.dk/historical-knowledge/denmark/prehistoric-period-until-1050-ad/the-viking-age/religion-magic-death-and-rituals/human-sacrifices/

National Museum Denmark. (2019b). *Runic magic - National Museum of Denmark*. National Museum of Denmark. https://en.natmus.dk/historical-knowledge/denmark/prehistoric-period-until-1050-ad/the-viking-age/religion-magic-death-and-rituals/runic-magic/

National Museum Denmark. (2019c). *The Viking blótss sacrifices - National Museum of Denmark*. National Museum of Denmark. https://en.natmus.dk/historical-knowledge/denmark/prehistoric-period-until-1050-ad/the-viking-age/religion-magic-death-and-rituals/the-viking-blótss-sacrifices/

National Museum Denmark. (2019d). *Viking seeresses - National Museum of Denmark*. National Museum of Denmark. https://en.natmus.dk/

historical-knowledge/denmark/prehistoric-period-until-1050-ad/the-viking-age/religion-magic-death-and-rituals/viking-seeresses/

National Museums Denmark. (2019). *The old Nordic religion today - National Museum of Denmark*. National Museum of Denmark. https://en.natmus.dk/historical-knowledge/denmark/prehistoric-period-until-1050-ad/the-viking-age/religion-magic-death-and-rituals/the-old-nordic-religion-today/

Nerthus. (2021, December 12). Wikipedia. https://en.wikipedia.org/wiki/Nerthus

Nikitins, T. (2017, September 4). *The Demonization of the Jötnar. Huginn's Heathen Hof.* http://www.heathenhof.com/demonization-Jötnar-modern-heathenry/

Nordic "Soul" Concepts. (n.d.). The Bone Kindred. Retrieved February 9, 2022, from http://bonekindred.weebly.com/nordic-soul-concepts.html

October 2020, T. M.-L. S. C. 08. (2020, October 8). *1,200-year-old pagan temple to Thor and Odin unearthed in Norway*. Livescience.com. https://www.livescience.com/ancient-viking-temple-to-thor-odin-unearthed.html

Ongkowidjojo, V. (2020, December 9). *The Northern Mysteries Current: Futhark and Mystery Schools of the Viking Age*. Www.ancient-Origins.net. https://www.ancient-origins.net/opinion-guest-authors/schools-viking-age-005971

Padraic Colum. (1984). *The children of Odin : the book of Northern myths* (Project Gutenberg eBook). Macmillan. https://www.gutenberg.org/files/24737/24737-h/24737-h.htm

Paxson, Diana. L. (2000). *Beloved: On Frigg and Her Handmaidens – Hrafnar*. Hrafnar.org. https://hrafnar.org/articles/dpaxson/asynjur/frigg/

Paxson, D. L. (1992). *Utgard: The Role of the Jötnar in the Religion of the North – Hrafnar*. Hrafnar.org. https://hrafnar.org/articles/dpaxson/norse/utgard/

Paxson, D. L. (1993). *The Return of the Völva: Recovering the Practice of Seiðr – Seeing for the People*. Seidh.org. https://seidh.org/articles/seidh/

Paxson, D. L. (1995). *Hyge-cræft: Working with the Soul in the Northern Tradition – Hrafnar*. Hrafnar.org. https://hrafnar.org/articles/dpaxson/norse/hyge-craeft/

Paxson, D. L. (1998). *Drumming with the Witches: Odin and Women's Wisdom – Hrafnar*. Hrafnar.org. https://hrafnar.org/articles/dpaxson

norse/odin-women/

Paxson, D. L. (2012a, April 9). *Earth-Religion and the Troth of the North – Hrafnar*. Hrafnar.org. https://hrafnar.org/articles/dpaxson/norse/hail-earth/

Paxson, D. L. (2012b, April 9). *Worshipping the Gods – Hrafnar*. Hrafnar. org. https://hrafnar.org/articles/dpaxson/norse/worship/

Phone, V. address M. of C. H. gate 2 0164 O. M. address P. O. B. 6762 S. O. plass 0130 O., & fax. (n.d.). *Kiss me – the world of runes - Museum of Cultural History*. Www.khm.uio.no. Retrieved February 7, 2022, from https://www.khm.uio.no/english/visit-us/historical-museum/exhibitions-archive/kiss-me-the-world-of-runes/

Price, N. (2002). Seidr. *In The Viking Way. Department of Archaeology and Ancient History Uppsala University*. https://yale.learningu.org/download/c03d3162-0caf-4750-a30f-1333a18c3ec2/C3339_Viking%20Way.pdf

Pruitt, S. (2019, June 27). *What We Know About Vikings and Slaves*. HISTORY. https://www.history.com/news/viking-slavery-raids-evidence

Ravynstar, D. (2012, May 14). *Goddess Sól. Journeying to the Goddess*. https://journeyingtothegoddess.wordpress.com/2012/05/14/goddess-sol/

Reaves, W. P. (2018). *Odin's Wife: Mother Earth in Germanic Mythology*. http://www.germanicmythology.com/original/SAMPLE_NERTHUS.pdf

Robertson, D. (1976). *Magical medicine in Viking Scandinavia*. Medical History, 20(3), 317–322. https://doi.org/10.1017/s0025727300022705

Rune poem. (2021, May 27). Wikipedia. https://en.wikipedia.org/wiki/Rune_poem

runeworker Br. Christopher. (2009, September 29). *Galdr and Taufr (spells and talismans)*. RUNEWORKER. https://runeworker.wordpress.com/2009/09/29/galdr-and-taufr-spells-and-talismans/

Sacred Space in the Lore and Modern Paganism. (n.d.). Www.englatheod.org. Retrieved February 3, 2022, from http://www.englatheod.org/sacredspace.htm

Saemund, Bray, O., & Ashliman, D. L. (n.d.). *Hávamál*. Sites.pitt.edu. https://sites.pitt.edu/~dash/havamal.html

Scott. (2019, February 10). *Saining not Smudging - Purification and Lustration in Scottish Folk Magic Practice*. Cailleach's Herbarium. https://cailleachs-herbarium.com/2019/02/saining-not-smudging-purification-and-lustration-in-scottish-folk-magic-practice/

Scribes, J. S. (2010a, September 27). *RUNES - Care, Cleansing, Empowering and Storage*. HubPages. https://discover.hubpages.com/religion-philosophy/RUNES-Care-Cleansing-Empowering-and-Storage

Scribes, J. S. (2010b, November 2). *RUNES: The RUNES and Their Meanings - 3 Aetts*. RUNES. http://elderfutharkrunes.blogspot.com/2010/11/runes-and-their-meanings-3-aetts.html

Seidhr. (n.d.). The Bone Kindred. Retrieved February 9, 2022, from http://bonekindred.weebly.com/seidhr.html

SEI. (2022, January 1). Wikipedia. https://en.wikipedia.org/wiki/Sei

Siikala, Anna-Leena. (1990). *Singing of incantations in Nordic tradition*. Scripta Instituti Donneriani Aboensis. 13. 191-205. 10.30674/scripta.67176.

Skjalden. (2018, March 11). *Völva the Viking Witch or Seeress*. Nordic Culture. https://skjalden.com/völvur-the-viking-witch-or-seeress/

Skogsberg, R. (2016, August 15). *Creating Sacred Space*. Huginn's Heathen Hof. http://www.heathenhof.com/creating-sacred-space/

Smith, C. (2017, March 2). *Frey – Norse Mythology and Religion*. Sites.psu.edu. https://sites.psu.edu/miamidolphins/2017/03/02/frey/

SnitchSeeker.com - View Single Post - Futhark Magic: A Study of Ancient Runes. (n.d.). Www.snitchseeker.com. Retrieved February 5, 2022, from https://www.snitchseeker.com/10113358-post8.html

solsdottir. (2015a, February 19). *So, who is Ullr? We Are Star Stuff*. https://earthandstarryheaven.com/2015/02/19/so-who-is-ullr/#more-445

solsdottir. (2015b, February 25). *2. Ship Burials, Stone Ships and the Afterlife. We Are Star Stuff*. https://earthandstarryheaven.com/2015/02/25/the-vanir-ship-burial-and-the-afterlife/#more-774

solsdottir. (2015c, April 17). *Heimdall v. Loki. We Are Star Stuff*. https://earthandstarryheaven.com/2015/04/17/heimdall-v-loki/

solsdottir. (2016, June 29). *The Golden Age: Njord and Saturn. We Are Star Stuff*. https://earthandstarryheaven.com/2016/06/29/njord-saturn/#more-12244

solsdottir. (2017a, January 11). *Njord: God of Peace and Plenty. We Are Star Stuff*. https://earthandstarryheaven.com/2017/01/11/njord/#more-14917

solsdottir. (2017b, March 16). *The Norns, Need and Fate. We Are Star Stuff*. https://earthandstarryheaven.com/2017/03/16/Norns/#more-15204

solsdottir. (2017c, May 24). *The Rest of the Vanir: overlooked goddesses, waves, and women. We Are Star Stuff*. https://earthandstarryheaven.com/2017/05/24/vanir-goddesses/#more-17083

solsdottir. (2017d, November 8). *The Powerful Dead*. *We Are Star Stuff*. https://earthandstarryheaven.com/2017/11/08/powerful-dead/#more-14770

solsdottir. (2017e, November 29). *Thor: ride the lightning*. *We Are Star Stuff*. https://earthandstarryheaven.com/2017/11/29/thor/#more-16751

solsdottir. (2017f, December 13). *Thor vs. Odin*. *We Are Star Stuff*. https://earthandstarryheaven.com/2017/12/13/thor-vs-odin/#more-18176

solsdottir. (2017g, December 21). *Sunna and the elves*. *We Are Star Stuff*. https://earthandstarryheaven.com/2017/12/21/sunna-elves/#more-13155

solsdottir. (2018, December 19). *The Vanir and their cult*. *We Are Star Stuff*. https://earthandstarryheaven.com/2018/12/19/vanir-cult/#more-13561

solsdottir. (2019a, April 25). *Frigg, Queen and Mother*. *We Are Star Stuff*. https://earthandstarryheaven.com/2019/04/25/frigg/#more-14755

solsdottir. (2019b, May 8). *Frigg's Racier Side? We Are Star Stuff*. https://earthandstarryheaven.com/2019/05/08/frigg-racier/#more-19955

Staff. (2018). *Asatrú, the old Norse Paganism is the fastest growing and largest non-Christian religion in Iceland*. Icelandmag. https://icelandmag.is/article/asatru-old-norse-paganism-fastest-growing-and-largest-non-christian-religion-iceland

Staff. (2019, January 22). *11 things to know about the present day practice of Asatrú, the ancient religion of the Vikings*. Icelandmag. https://icelandmag.is/article/11-things-know-about-present-day-practice-asatru-ancient-religion-vikings

Stone, R., & Winters, R. (2020, April 11). *Vestiges of the Vikings: Magic Buried in a Viking Woman's Grave*. Www.ancient-Origins.net. https://www.ancient-origins.net/artifacts-other-artifacts/vestiges-vikings-magic-buried-viking-womans-grave-006800

Storesund, E. (2017, May 1). *Sex, drugs, and drop-spindles: What is Seiðr? (Norse metaphysics pt. 2)*. Brute Norse. https://www.brutenorse.com/blog/2017/05/sex-drugs-and-drop-spindles-what-is.html

Storyteller, R. (2008, March 30). *Rune Shamanism: Rune Shamanism Galdr Chants*. Rune Shamanism. http://runeshamanism.blogspot.com/2008/03/rune-shamanism-galdr-chants.html

The Editors of the Encyclopedia Britannica. (2021, August 25). *Tyr | Germanic deity*. Encyclopedia Britannica. https://www.britannica.com/topic/Tyr

The mythological world of the Vikings | The Swedish History Museum. (n.d.). Historiska.se. https://historiska.se/norse-mythology/mythological-world-of-the-vikings/

The Norse Witch, M. (2018, December 22). *Oðin. Máni - the Norse Witch.* https://theheart756621753.wordpress.com/odin/

The Norwegian Rune Poem, English Translation. (n.d.). Www.ragweedforge.com. Retrieved February 11, 2022, from https://www.ragweedforge.com/RunNRPe.html

The Viking Way (book). (2021, October 30). Wikipedia. https://en.wikipedia.org/wiki/The_Viking_Way_(book)

Thorpe, B., Blackwell, I. A., Anderson, R. B., & Buel, J. W. (1911). *The Elder Edda of Saemund Sigfusson.* Norrœna Society. https://www.gutenberg.org/files/14726/14726-h/14726-h.htm

T. (2020, May 10). Wikipedia. https://en.wikipedia.org/wiki/T

Towrie, S. (n.d.-a). *Orkneyjar - The Odin Oath.* Www.orkneyjar.com. Retrieved February 5, 2022, from http://www.orkneyjar.com/history/odinstone/odinoath.htm

Towrie, S. (n.d.-b). *Orkneyjar - The Odin Stone.* Www.orkneyjar.com. Retrieved February 5, 2022, from http://www.orkneyjar.com/history/odinstone/tradition.htm

Towrie, S. (n.d.-c). *Witchcraft in the Orkney Isles: The Development of the Orkney Witch.* Www.orkneyjar.com. Retrieved February 5, 2022, from http://www.orkneyjar.com/folklore/witchcraft/sorcery.htm

Towrie, S. (n.d.-d). Witchcraft in the Orkney Isles: The Spae Wife. Www.orkneyjar.com. Retrieved February 10, 2022, from http://www.orkneyjar.com/folklore/witchcraft/spaewife.htm

Towrie, S. (n.d.-e). *Witchcraft in the Orkney Isles: The Spae Wife.* Www.orkneyjar.com. Retrieved February 10, 2022, from http://www.orkneyjar.com/history/maeshowe/maeshrunes.htm

Twofeathers, S. (n.d.). *Incantation | Magickal Ingredients.* Shirleytwofeathers.com. Retrieved February 5, 2022, from https://shirleytwofeathers.com/The_Blog/magickal-ingredients/tag/incantation/

Ullr. (2020, August 13). Wikipedia. https://en.wikipedia.org/wiki/Ullr

Valda Roric. (2019, May 19). *Decoding Viking Signs: Nine Norse Symbols Explained.* Www.ancient-Origins.net. https://www.ancient-origins.net/myths-legends/decoding-ancient-symbols-norsemen-005951

Viktor Rydberg, & Anderson, R. B. (1906a). *Teutonic Mythology: Vol. One*. London. https://www.gutenberg.org/files/37876/37876-h/37876-h.htm

Viktor Rydberg, & Anderson, R. B. (1906b). *Teutonic Mythology: Vol. Three*. London. https://www.gutenberg.org/files/58830/58830-h/58830-h.htm

Viktor Rydberg, & Anderson, R. B. (1906c). *Teutonic Mythology: Vol. Two*. London. https://www.gutenberg.org/files/58829/58829-h/58829-h.htm

Ward, Christie. L. (n.d.). *Viking Answer Lady Webpage - Women and Magic in the Sagas: Seiðr and Spá*. Www.vikinganswerlady.com. http://www.vikinganswerlady.com/seidhr.shtml

Wikipedia Contributors. (2019a, May 1). *Thor*. Wikipedia; Wikimedia Foundation. https://en.wikipedia.org/wiki/Thor

Wikipedia Contributors. (2019b, May 5). *Jötunn*. Wikipedia; Wikimedia Foundation. https://en.wikipedia.org/wiki/J

Wikipedia Contributors. (2019c, May 8). *Hallucinogen*. Wikipedia; Wikimedia Foundation. https://en.wikipedia.org/wiki/Hallucinogen

Wikipedia Contributors. (2019d, May 10). *Baldr*. Wikipedia; Wikimedia Foundation. https://en.wikipedia.org/wiki/Baldr

Wikipedia Contributors. (2019e, September 23). *S*. Wikipedia; Wikimedia Foundation. https://en.wikipedia.org/wiki/S

Wikipedia Contributors. (2019f, October 25). *Freyr*. Wikipedia; Wikimedia Foundation. https://en.wikipedia.org/wiki/Freyr

Worship of the Jotun? (2018, May 18). Religious Forums. https://www.religiousforums.com/threads/worship-of-the-jotun.213421/

Yngling. (2021, December 3). Wikipedia. https://en.wikipedia.org/wiki/Yngling

www.ingramcontent.com/pod-product-compliance
Lightning Source LLC
Chambersburg PA
CBHW071856160426
43209CB00005B/1073